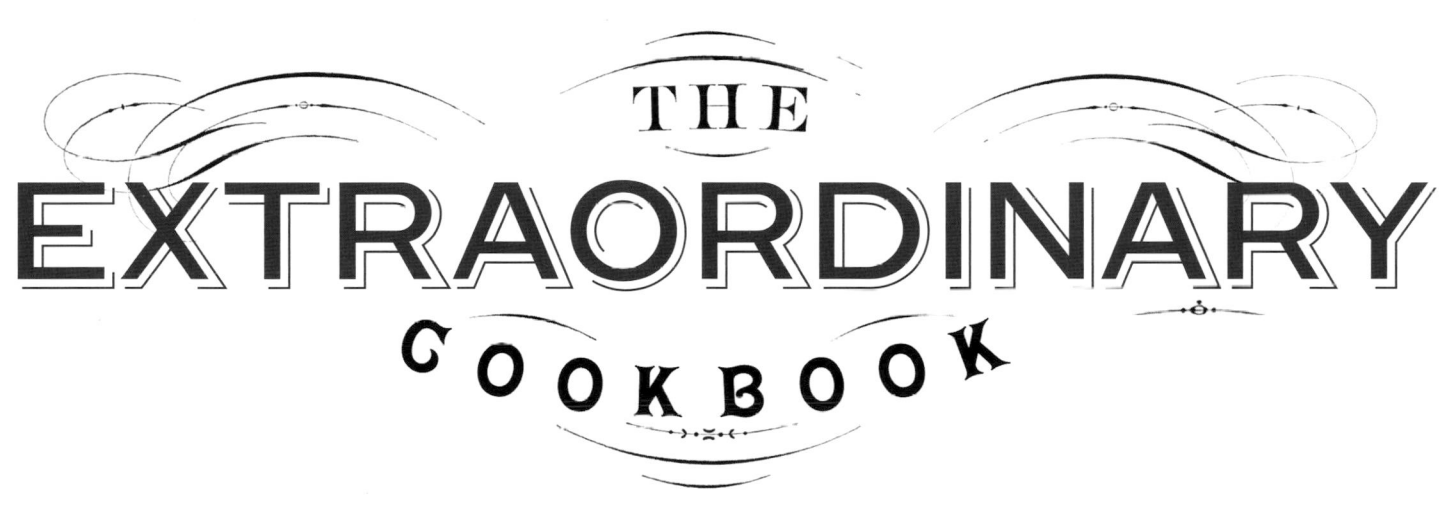

THE EXTRAORDINARY COOKBOOK

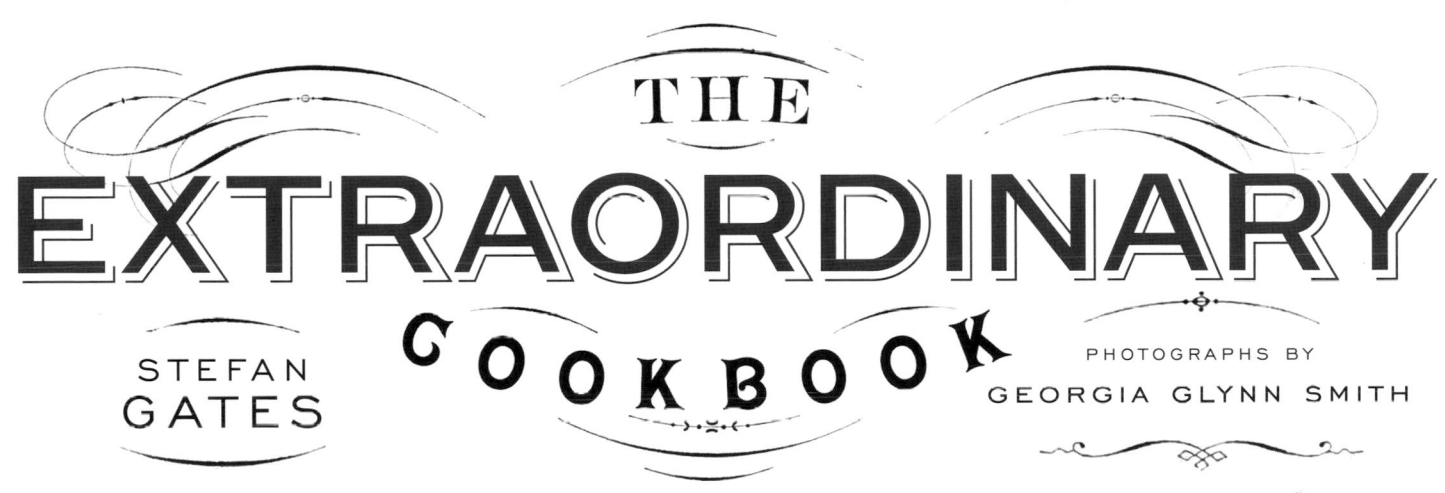

THE EXTRAORDINARY COOKBOOK

STEFAN GATES

PHOTOGRAPHS BY
GEORGIA GLYNN SMITH

HOW TO MAKE
MEALS YOUR
FRIENDS
WILL
NEVER
FORGET

KYLE CATHIE LIMITED

To Poppy, Daisy and Georgia
For making it all so much fun

To you
For joining in

~~~~~~

First published in Great Britain in 2010 by
Kyle Cathie Limited
23 Howland Street, London W1T 4AY
general.enquiries@kyle-cathie.com
www.kylecathie.com

10 9 8 7 6 5 4 3 2 1

ISBN 978-1-85626-921-6

Project editor: Jenny Wheatley
Photographer: Georgia Glynn Smith
Designer: Two Associates
Food stylist: Marina Filippelli
Props stylist: Lyndsay Milne Mcleod
Copy editor: Anne McDowall
Editorial assistant: Elanor Clarke
Production: Gemma John

A Cataloguing In Publication record for this title is available from the British Library.

Printed in China by C & C offset Printing Co.

CONTENTS

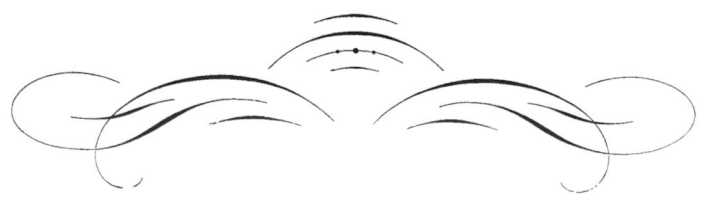

HELLO

I have two humble ambitions in writing this book:

1. To blow your mind.
2. To transform your meals into adventures.

Despite what you might think, it's actually pretty easy to create meals that your friends will never forget. You don't need to spend lots of time or money but you do need some inspiration and a little handholding, and that's what this book is for. All the recipes here are practical and thoroughly achievable – nothing is included simply as a flight of fancy or to make the book look impressive, and although you might save a few of these dishes for a special occasion, the vast majority are meals that I make on a daily basis at home. Hang on, there is the obvious exception of liquid nitrogen ice cream which, it's true, is an indulgent frippery. But that's about it.

There are a few dishes that sound challenging such as Apple Caviar, Crispy Jellyfish and Beansprout Salad and Kebabs Cooked on a Car Engine, but I urge you not to underestimate your family and friends' tolerance for adventures, and your ability to create them. You'll be surprised how even the pickiest eaters (especially kids) jump at the chance of an exhilarating culinary escapade, and that despite appearances, even dishes such as Golden Chicken can be easy and relatively cheap to make.

Often the key to unlocking the exhilaration in food is to re-think the way it's cooked and served. Can you get your friends to take part in the process? Can they interact with their food, perhaps in a way that they haven't before, by churning their own butter in a jam jar, by rolling their own sushi, by creating their own soup or by trying an ingredient like jellyfish that they'd never normally eat? Because that's the key to giving your friends an enlightening and unforgettable experience: by flattering their intelligence and feeding their appetite for adventure.

My favourite meals in this book are probably the ones in which my friends get thoroughly (often messily) involved. Every single time I've thrown a sushi rolling night, shabu-shabu feast or hammer-and-crab riot, the evening is transformed from a dinner into a party. When people really get to grips with their food they have a sensual as well as social experience and they lose their inhibitions. And that, my friends, is all you need: the rest of your adventure will follow as a matter of course.

Sharing food is vital to my happiness and I'm sure it is to yours. Whether you make Chicken Liver Parfait, Vegetable Instruments or Fluorescent Jellies, whether you serve a simple bowl of peas still in their pods or the world's finest bellota jamón Iberico, I truly believe that unforgettable and extraordinary meals shared with the people you love are the some of the most wonderful experiences life has to offer.

I've had a fantastic time writing this book. I really hope you enjoy it and that it leads you to some extraordinary experiences. If it does, I want to know all about them. Drop me a line at www.thegastronaut.com

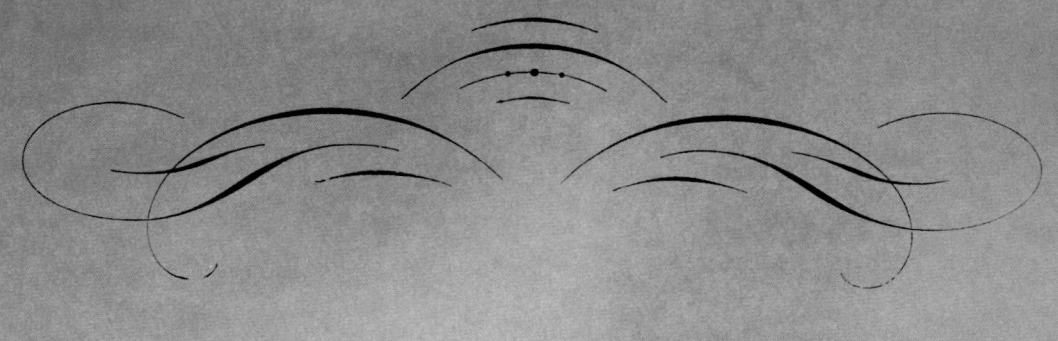

1

SNACKS

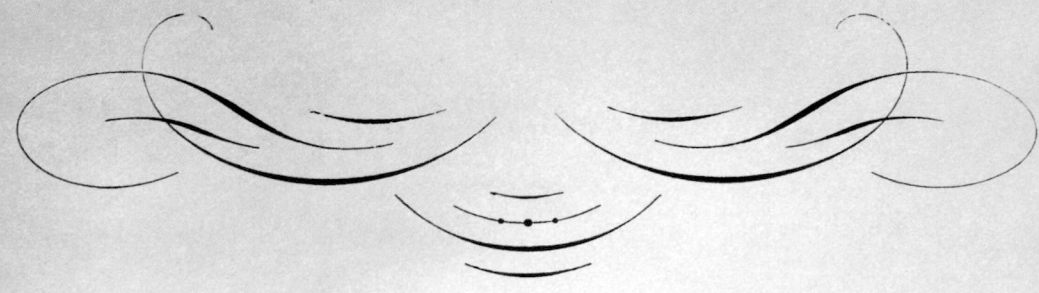

I LIKE DINNERS AT MY HOUSE TO BE relaxed but exhilarating affairs, so when you come over for supper you'll inevitably arrive to merry chaos, with the kids up way too late (refusing to go to bed until they've met you), loud music on the stereo, my head in the oven (in a good way) and little samples of food all over the place because I wanted you to try something new that I've found. Likely as not, you'll be roped in to read the kids a story, toast some chestnuts, carve a butternut bassoon or whittle a radish mouse. This might sound a bit slack, but there's a good reason for it: I want you to feel involved and relaxed and I don't want you to spend a single moment worrying what you're going to say or who you're going to sit next to. I do have two unbreakable rules, for myself to follow: the table must be laid (I want you to feel welcome and expected), and there should always be some snacks to pick at. Little nuggets of magical tastes and little bombs of flavour or possibly something extraordinary or adventurous to get your taste buds tickled-up. These are foods to eat with your hands, to get you licking your fingers and to warm you up for the adventures to come. I want you to drop your defences, to prime yourself for adventure and get ready for a meal that you'll never forget.

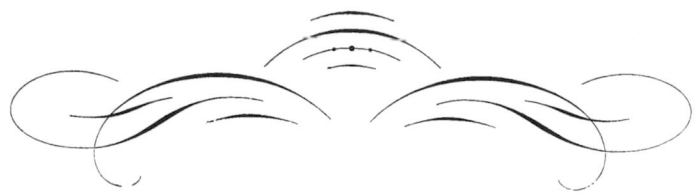

BLOODY MARY TOMATOES

Be very careful when you hand these around as they are disarmingly tasty and sneakily alcoholic. They are also perfectly bite-sized, so you'll find yourself popping them into your mouth one after the other like grapes, and before you know it, you and your friends will be utterly legless.

The following story is a salutary lesson – and too funny to keep to myself. A few years ago we held a big lunch party after my daughter's christening, and the lovely vicar kindly agreed to come along, accompanied by the equally lovely lady preacher. Anyone who thought their presence might add a little gravity to the situation was to be sorely disappointed, however. It all started when the Bloody Mary tomatoes came out, and both vicar and preacher tucked in with great enthusiasm. It's *possible* that I forgot to mention that the tomatoes were packed with vodka, but anyone could have been forgiven for thinking that they were just very tasty. And of course, vodka can be strangely hard to detect, especially when you've got a glass of wine in the other hand.

Anyway, both vicar and preacher enjoyed the tomatoes enormously, so much so that by the time they sat down to eat they were already slurring their words. The vicar struck up a ferocious theological argument with the preacher and before long I heard him use a phrase that was, well, let's just say it was very naughty. Upon hearing himself utter said phrase, it dawned on him that perhaps it was time to leave. He and the preacher thanked us all profusely and ambled out. A few moments later, we heard an enormous crash, and we all raced out to the hallway to find the vicar and the preacher rolling on the floor in fits of giggles, having knocked a large picture off the wall. Luckily, damage was done to neither property nor priest, so I gave them both a hug and sent them wandering off down the street.

SERVES 6

30 ripe cherry tomatoes (about 800g), the tastiest you can find
400ml good vodka
50ml sherry (optional – if you don't have any, replace with vodka)
1 tablespoon Worcester sauce
1 teaspoon Tabasco
1 teaspoon grated fresh horseradish (optional)
4 fresh thyme sprigs (optional)
celery salt and plain salt, to serve

Prick each tomato several times using a cocktail stick. In a bowl, mix together the vodka, sherry, Worcester sauce, Tabasco, horseradish and thyme.

Place the tomatoes in a large jar (or several small jars) then pour over the marinade until they are covered. (If necessary, add a little more vodka so that all are submerged.) Leave for at least 2 days. The tomatoes get a little wizened and over-alcoholic after a few weeks, and by the time they are a month old they are over the hill and should be blitzed with chopped tomatoes to make a stonking Bloody Mary.

Serve the tomatoes with a small dipping bowl of equal measures of celery salt mixed with plain salt.

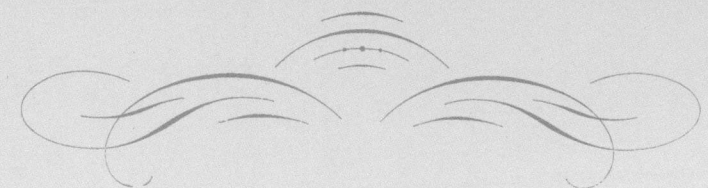

BOWLS OF PEA PODS OR EDAMAME BEANS

It's not exactly a recipe, is it? But when you place a bowl of pea pods on the table for your friends to tuck into, something small but revelatory happens. Your friends start their meal by touching something organic rather than metallic – food rather than fork – and they immediately interact with it (if that's not too grand a word for 'fiddling'). Of course, you could just get your guests to do some work for you by shelling peas to accompany the main course. (I always like to hand out a few tasks like this as it gets people chatting at the start of an evening.)

EDAMAME BEANS

Unlike pea pods, edamame (pronounced 'ed–a-mahmay') are best cooked before serving. They are green soy beans, and you can buy them frozen from Japanese and Chinese stores in 1kg bags.

If you've bought frozen beans, check the packet to see if they've been cooked before freezing; they usually have. If they've been pre-cooked, just throw them in a large pan of boiling water and as soon as the water comes back to a boil, drain. If they have been frozen raw, or if you have bought fresh beans, throw them into a large pan of boiling water, bring back to the boil and simmer for 3–4 minutes before draining. Sprinkle the cooked beans with salt and soy sauce before serving.

RUSSIAN ROULETTE PADRÓN PEPPERS

These beautiful little peppers, about the size of a thumb, are fantastic to serve as a snack alongside a glass of chilled manzanilla or oloroso sherry. However, it's not just their taste that makes them extraordinary but also the fact that around one in twelve of them are hot enough to give you an exciting jolt of capsaicin (the active ingredient in chillies).

They are traditionally grown around the village of Padrón in Galicia, northwestern Spain, although you can now find them all over the world, and the seeds are widely available, so you can even grow them in your garden (see Suppliers, page 218). Debate rages over the proportion of hot peppers in each batch, some people claiming 1:10 and others 1:50. I've eaten them when every other one seems to have a big chilli kick, but when I staged a game of Russian roulette peppers on a TV show, not a single one turned out to be hot, much to my annoyance. It didn't really matter, though, because they were so sweet and complex in flavour that their deliciousness made up for it.

SERVES 6

375g bag of Padrón peppers
(often sold as *pimientos de Padrón*)
3 tablespoons olive oil
salt (preferably in flaky crystals)

Heat the olive oil in a large frying pan, then fry the peppers a large handful at a time, until the skins start to blister and brown. Be careful though: they can spit and pop in the oil. Remove, rest on a paper towel to remove any excess oil, scatter liberally with sea salt and serve hot.

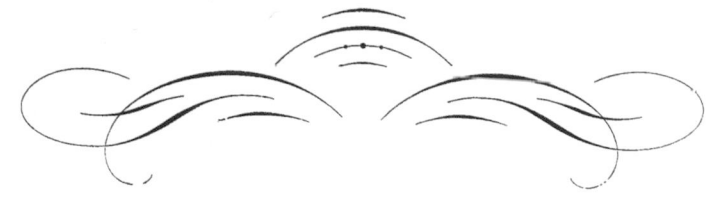

RADISH MICE

The extraordinary design of the radish, with the contrast between its livid fuchsia outer skin and pure white innards, meant that it was only a matter of time before people started using it for art. The classic book on food fiddling like this is the wonderfully bonkers, slightly twisted German *Du Mont's Phantasievoller Ratgeber für Vergnugte Koche* (Imaginative Guide for the Happy Cook).

Use super-fresh radishes and keep them in the fridge until you serve them to stop them going droopy. These mice are great as a little snack before dinner, but also to accompany a plate of cheese. It might sound a little naff, but if your friends are cool enough to play, it's fun to let people make their own mice.

Wash the radishes, but leave the stringy 'tail' on and cut the greenery off to leave behind a stubby green nose and maybe a few whiskers. Cut a base off each radish (this will help it stay upright) and then cut two small discs from that base offcut for ears. Make two small nicks in the head end of the radish and stick the ears into them. Spike some eye-socket holes with the prong of a fork, then push two peppercorns in to form the eyes. Store the mice in the fridge until needed. Warning: don't eat the peppercorns!

RADISHES AND ALMONDS WITH SALT

Radishes have a lovely hot bite to them, and they are delicious scrubbed and eaten just as they are, dipped in salt. The same works for almonds, and if you ever manage to find young almonds still in their green shells (or can scrump a few from a tree), you will be able to treat yourself to a little slice of heaven. Crack the shells open (a strong set of teeth would do it) and pick out the creamy nut inside, then dip in the tiniest amount of salt crystals.

SERVES 6

2 bunches of fresh radishes
2 handfuls of fresh almonds or walnuts
    (if in season, optional)
sea salt, for dipping

Pull the larger leaves off the radishes, leaving some stalk behind. Wash and drain. Serve (with the almonds if you managed to find them) with a small pot of salt for dipping.

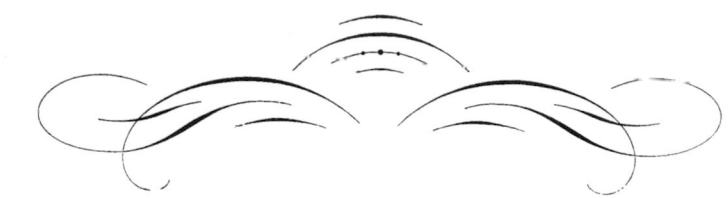

PICKLED EGG IN A BAG OF CRISPS

My friend Nick often serves this The Drapers Arms, which just happens to be my favourite pub. There's something exhilaratingly childish about being given a pickled egg, a bag of crisps and the licence to squish them together to make a gloriously heady, vinegary mess.

This does seem to be mainly (although not exclusively) a boy thing, and an early 80s boy thing at that. Ignore the disapproving glances of wife/girlfriend (or husband/boyfriend, should you be bucking the trend) and open up a tangy bag of salt and vinegar crisps. Drop the pickled egg inside and gently squish the bag so that the egg breaks up but doesn't entirely disintegrate. Then sit back, hold pint of beer in one hand and tuck into the packet without an ounce of shame.

PICKLING YOUR OWN EGGS

a large jar
eggs (as many as will fit into your jar)
4 bay leaves
6 garlic cloves, peeled
malt vinegar
1 teaspoon black peppercorns

Put the eggs into a saucepan of cold water, bring to the boil and simmer for about 7 minutes (but for no longer than 10 minutes or the yolks will go grey inside). Transfer to a large pan of cold water to cool them and stop them from overcooking.

Crack the shells, peel the eggs and add them to the jar with the bay leaves and garlic. Pour over enough malt vinegar to cover them and then sprinkle the peppercorns on top. Seal the jars and label them with the date. You can eat them within 2 days, although they are best left for 2 weeks and can be eaten anything up to one year later.

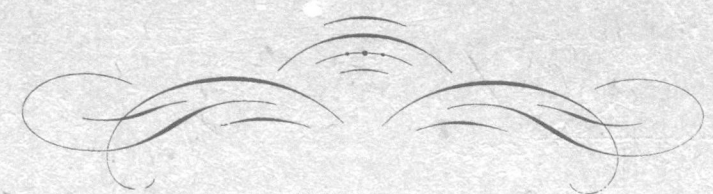

COCKTAIL STICK CANAPÉS FOR THE EXTRAORDINARY WORLD

The word 'canapé' always reminds me of pineapple and cheese on a cocktail stick, jabbed into a foil-covered potato and served in an *Abigail's Party*esque belief that it's the height of sophistication. I know I'm supposed to think that's naff, but I'm a product of the 70s, and I have to admit that I really like the fruit-cheese combination. So, here are a few ideas for updating the whole foil-covered potato hedgehog thing.

- Blue Stilton with ripe pear cubes (tossed in a little lemon juice to stop them from going brown).

- Lancashire cheese with cubes of Christmas cake (believe me, this really is fantastic, like the classic combination of Lancashire cheese and Eccles cake).

- Manchego with a little square of membrillo (quince cheese or paste).

- Cubes of Parmesan on their own, with a little bowl of balsamic vinegar to dip them into.

- Strong Cheddar with apple cubes (tossed in a little lemon juice to stop them from going brown). Go on, call me old-fashioned.

HOT TOASTED ALMONDS

It's a simple idea, but a plate of nuts that have been quickly roasted in the oven provides a hit of really good flavours, and combined with a glass of good sherry, it's a sparkling way to start an evening.

300g whole almonds, skins on
2 tablespoons olive oil
1 teaspoon sweet smoked paprika (optional)
1 teaspoon flaky salt crystals

Preheat the oven to 180°C. Put the almonds, olive oil and paprika together in a bowl and mix around so the almonds are all nicely coated in oil and spice, then spread them out on a roasting tray.

Roast them in the oven for 20 minutes, giving them a stir every five minutes. Remove from the oven to a sheet of kitchen paper to remove any excess oil, then sprinkle them with salt to taste. Serve with chilled manzanilla or oloroso sherry.

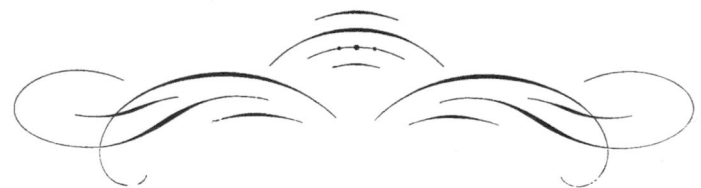

THAI-FLAVOURED OYSTERS SERVED IN A SPOON

These are ridiculously good. You can, of course, serve them in the oyster shell if you fancy, but there's something fun about using these Asian flat-bottomed spoons as mini bowls.

A WORD ON OYSTER SHUCKING

Opening oysters really doesn't have to be painful and difficult. If you manage to buy oysters with relatively flat, regular lips (the lip is the wide end of the oyster as opposed to the pointy end), you should be able to slip a flat butter knife through the thin shell from the lip end with minimal damage to the oyster. Here's a remarkably effective method I learned from a friend in France (change indicated hands if you're left-handed):

Place a tea-towel across your upturned left hand, then place the oyster on your covered palm with the flatter side up and the pointy end facing away from you. Gripping the sides of the oyster, and with your hand resting on a sturdy surface, dig a flat butter knife into the top edge of the lip nearest you and through into the cavity of the oyster. You should be able to do this without causing much damage at all, as long as your oysters are relatively flat-lipped.

Gently wriggle the knife into the oyster, keeping the blade at the top of the interior, then slice across from right to left to cut the main muscle that keeps the oyster shut. You may have to do some digging around for the first one, until you get the hang of it.

Prise the top shell off, then spill the smallest splash of the oyster's juices out of the shell and across the cut that you made to the shell to wash any stray bits of shell away.

Gently cut under the oyster flesh to release it from the lower shell.

If your oysters are rough and gnarly-looking you might have to resort to going in from the pointy end using a strong, pointier knife, but this generally causes more damage.

MAKES 12 SPOONS

1 spring onion, finely sliced
1 lemongrass stalk, outer leaves
    removed, very finely sliced
1 teaspoon Thai fish sauce (nam pla)
1 teaspoon toasted sesame oil
1 tablespoon vegetable oil
½ clove garlic, very finely chopped
½ chilli, seeds removed and
    very finely chopped
zest and juice of 1 lime
zest and juice of ½ orange
a handful of coriander leaves,
    finely chopped
12 medium-sized rock oysters

Put all the ingredients except the oysters together in a bowl and stir to combine (or put in a jam jar and shake vigorously). Set aside to infuse for half an hour while you prepare your oysters.

Shuck the oysters as described above, then remove the oysters from the shells and place one in each spoon or oyster shell. Sit the spoons on a tray that will fit in your fridge. Spoon over the infused sauce and store in the fridge until ready to serve.

TIP: if you're serving them in oyster shells, serve them on a bed of crushed ice or rock salt to keep them upright.

CHARCUTERIE

My kids love French *saucisson sec* with such a passion that I have to lock it away from them as they'll inevitably hoover the whole lot up if left unattended.

It's a great idea to invest in a small selection of good charcuterie to keep on the go, and just slice a few very thin slivers from each sausage as needed to lay on a wooden chopping board alongside some olives or toasted almonds. Charcuterie translates as 'cooked meats' (which is slightly misleading as most hams, saucisson and salami are cured in salt then air-dried without ever being cooked using heat).

Charcuterie makes a great appetiser, especially when the flavours of the supper you're planning are good and robust (I wouldn't serve it before sushi as the saltiness and intensity of the flavours will blow away the delicacy of the fish). Store your sausages in the fridge. There are some excellent varieties available, and you can get some wonderful combinations of pork with figs, nuts, wild boar, venison and the like. My favourite is a French one called *figuetel* made with extra pig's liver, which is extraordinarily intense.

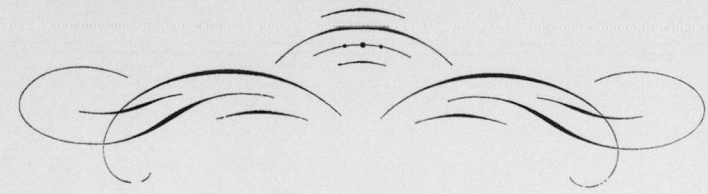

FOR THE LOVE OF JAMÓN

Whole legs and shoulders of air-cured ham make me go weak at the knees, and I usually have at least one on the go at home. You can buy basic, relatively inexpensive ones that are perfectly enjoyable or you can spend a king's ransom on a superb Joselito Gran Reserva Bellota acorn-fed Pata Negra and fly to gustatory heaven on a nightly basis. A cured ham is not that expensive when you consider that it will last a good few months and supply you with dozens of meals, and the flavour is so intense that you only need a few slices to feel as though you've eaten a feast. A whole leg of ham on the bone is a beautiful thing to behold, too. I'll often put the whole thing in front of a friend who arrives early for supper and set them to work cutting thin slivers of it. Choose one of your more dexterous mates and a long, firm ultra-sharp knife. This ham is mind-blowingly good when nibbled with a glass of manzanilla sherry.

If you do invest in a whole leg of cured ham, you'll need to buy or make a sturdy little stand for it otherwise it'll be a pain to carve. I have a few stands that came free with the legs, and although the kitchen-kit tart in me does yearn for the Jamotec J4 (the dream machine of ham stands) you certainly don't have to splash out on an expensive one. The cheaper ones (see Suppliers, page 218) will last for years, and a bit of sturdy DIY might also suffice, as long as it has a grip to hold the hoof and a good spike for the meaty end to sit on.

STORING A WHOLE LEG OF HAM

If your ham arrives vacuum-sealed it will last unopened for about six months kept in a cool place. Once opened, wipe any moisture and natural mould off and store it in a cool place, ideally at around 10–15°C. It should last for three months, although it gradually dries out. If you can, try to get a bone-in ham, rather than a boned one, as the latter will lose its structure after you've cut three-quarters of the meat off. If you have bought a boned ham, it's probably best kept in the fridge (if you've got one big enough).

Once you've started cutting into the ham, save a few large flat slices of fat to lay over the exposed meat, to slow down the drying-out process, and cover this with a dry tea-towel.

A LITTLE SECRET…

While writing this piece I got very excited about Pata Negra (Iberian blackfoot) ham, which is so expensive that I normally buy only a few slices a few times a year as a special treat. A whole Pata Negra leg costs about the same as a decent second-hand car, but I've discovered that you can also buy shoulders, which are less costly, from the great Pata Negra producers (see Suppliers, page 218). They have less meat and a little more connective tissue but they still have that all-important depth of flavour and long lingering delightful aftertaste of the real thing. Even a shoulder isn't exactly what you'd call cheap, but there's still a little cash left over for the kids' shoes – if they leave any ham for me, that is. And here's another tip: I tend to get my little daughter to click the final 'order' button on the website. That way I can blame her for splashing so much cash.

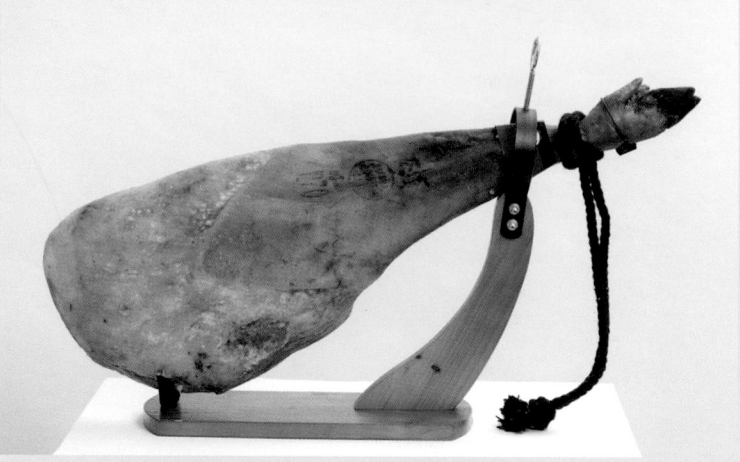 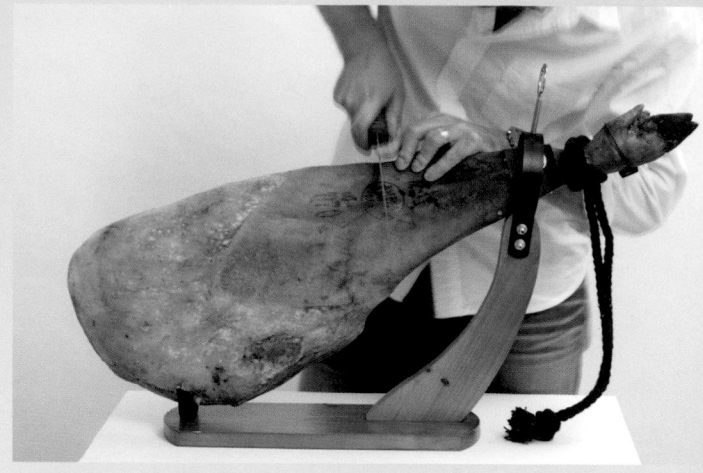

HOW TO CUT A WHOLE LEG OF HAM

I favour the Spanish method of cutting short thin slivers about 5cm long rather than trying to cut pieces the length of the ham. It's easier to eat, and it makes the whole process less stressful! Place the leg in a stand with the back of the hoof facing up (i.e. with the front of the calf facing downwards).

Using a short, sharp knife, cut the skin and fat off around the top of the leg to reveal the meat inside (keep the fat for cooking with). This is the fiddly bit, and there's a fair amount of pulling and hacking as the skin is tough, but once you're in, it gets much easier.

Now cut the fat from the top of the leg in a few large flat pieces, if you can, reserving it for protecting the exposed meat from drying out. When you get down to the meat, begin carving across in small pieces, whittling down until you start getting small slices about 5cm long, cutting from

the hoof end towards the thigh, and keeping the fatty edges on each piece (they are to be eaten too). Try to keep the surface flat where you can. You'll need to cut around the pelvic bone or shoulder blade when you get to it, but don't try to cut these bones out – it's too destructive. Cut away more of the skin as you need to, and when you've cut every bit from one side, turn the leg over and start on the other side.

You can't eat much from around the hock end, but save it to make an extraordinary, intensely flavoured ham and pea soup. Be warned, though: the ham has been heavily salted before drying, so don't add any salt to your soup until you're sure it's needed.

After each carving session, cover the exposed meat with fat or greaseproof paper and cover that with a tea-towel and store somewhere cool.

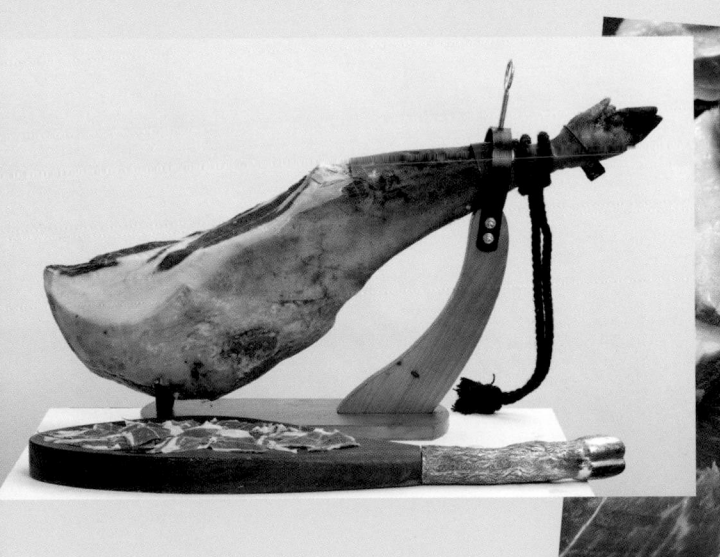

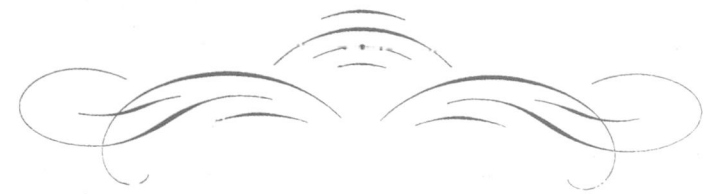

HOLEY-PAN-ROASTED CHESTNUTS

The smell of roasting chestnuts reminds me of Christmas far more than pine, chocolate or spice. I remember eating these as a kid walking down London's Oxford Street in the falling snow, wrapped up in layers of wool against the bitter cold and desperately wishing that I could be taken to Hamleys, but warmed by a charred handful of pungent chestnuts.

When you buy these on Oxford Street, they are usually roasted on a brazier, and their smell is their best advert. I always thought it would be impossible to get that smell at home, but when I met my wife, she showed me her rusty pans (an unconventional courting move, to be sure). They had holes drilled in them. I initially thought they were improvised colanders, but of course, they were chestnut-roasting pans, and very beautiful they are too.

THE HOLEY-PAN METHOD

Use this method for open fires, gas hobs, bonfires or barbecues. Pick up an old uncoated metal pan from your second-hand shop (or sacrifice an exhausted one of your own), and drill lots of holes in it, about the width of a pencil.

Cut little crosses into the chestnuts, either on the sides or at the base. This is to stop them from exploding, which is highly likely to happen unless you give the steam a route to escape.

Place the chestnuts in a holey pan and place the pan over a fire. (This method also works happily over a normal gas hob.) Supervise the pan throughout cooking, shaking it every now and then to prevent the chestnuts from burning too much – you want them to char but not burn to a cinder.

It will take around 10–20 minutes for them to cook, depending on size of nut and heat of flame, during which time the nominated cook – not your good self, as you'll probably be elsewhere cooking something extraordinary – should be plied with glasses of port. Test one for tenderness and then leave the whole lot to cool a little before serving with some salt.

OVEN METHOD

Preheat the oven to 200°C. Cut little crosses on the chestnuts as described above, then place in a roasting tin and cook uncovered for 20–30 minutes.

Roasted chestnuts are best eaten still warm to the touch and peeled by the eater themselves. We like dipping them in a little pot of salt crystals.

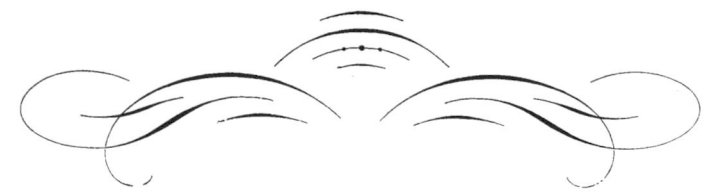

WEIRD AND WONDERFUL SNACKS (1): CHINATOWN

I love taking my friends on culinary adventures when they come over to play, so whenever I visit Chinese or Thai shops I keep an eye out for something new that might tickle their fancy. I picked up the selection in the photo opposite on a visit to Chinatown, but you can also find most of these online (see Suppliers, page 218). Wasabi peas are always great (they sometimes have quite a kick), and you can usually find all manner of sticky rice bun thingies, but the best fun is to be had when the packets aren't translated and you haven't a clue what you've let yourself in for!

INSTANT DIM SUM FUN

This is the epitome of lazy extraordinary food. We eat frozen ready-made dumplings at my house whenever we need an emergency feast, or when we've been so greedy over a weekend that there's nothing left in the fridge come Monday. Don't let the fact that they're frozen put you off – dumplings freeze really well, and they taste great. I keep a selection of them in the freezer: loads of basic prawn, vegetable, pork and chicken gyoza-style dumplings to fill me up and a few of the more delicate *har kau* open-topped ones for steaming.

The Cantonese phrase *dim sum* refers not to a specific food but to a way of eating. It translates as 'close to the heart', and refers to any range of snacks and nibbles and tasters that you fancy. Dumplings are probably the most common, although chicken feet and duck's tongues are very popular too.

There are two usual methods for cooking frozen dumplings: the delicate open-topped ones and the big fat buns just need to be steamed (usually for about 8 minutes or so), while the gyoza-style ones need to be very gently simmered from frozen first (the water has to boil very gently otherwise the pastry casings can split), and then drained and finished off in a frying pan with some vegetable oil to lightly brown them. Check the instructions on the packet, although be warned: they are often translated into English a little oddly. Serve with soy or ponzu sauce and eat with chopsticks.

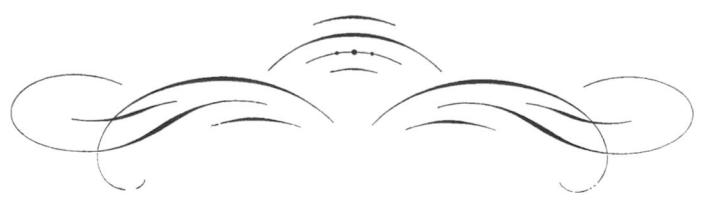

COCHINEAL

This isn't a recipe, it's a diversion. Because it just struck me that you probably thought you weren't an entomophagist (insect-eater) when the reality is that bugs crop up in our food whether we want them to or not. The Food and Drug Administration allows up to 150 insect fragments in each 100g of flour, in what amounts to an admission of the inevitability of their presence in our grub. Basically, anyone who eats natural food is likely to munch a few bits and bobs of bugs without ever thinking about it. And of course there's honey, which is, let's face it, bee-regurgitated nectar.

But bugs are often put in your food as an ingredient, too. If you've ever eaten sausages, liquorice allsorts, M & Ms, or indeed a pink sweet of any description, you are highly likely to have eaten the little crinkly purple nibs in the photo opposite. Those little fellas are dried cochineal bugs that I harvested and dried myself on a resurrected cochineal farm in Lanzarote (the industry is dormant on the island because South American countries currently produce it more cheaply). When you see 'cochineal', 'carmine' or E120 listed on the label of any food, what you've got is a tiny amount of those bugs ground into a pink or purple dye.

Cochineal bugs are little scale insects each about the size of a peppercorn, which grow on cactus leaves in Lanzarote and some South American countries, with the world's main commercial production in Peru. Thousands of acres are planted with cacti specifically for the purpose of cochineal production and the bugs look like grey, mouldy, scrofulous carbuncles clinging on to the cactus leaves as they grow. But under their grey covering the bugs have a deep crimson-purple colouring, and when you crush a live one in your palm, they burst with an explosion of deeply coloured blood that's so intense that it stains your hands and clothes on contact.

Cochineal is popular with food manufacturers because it's an organic product (so it can be labelled 'natural') and it's very stable, unlike some dyes that can often fade over time. It can be used as a simple ground powder of the dried insects, or a more intense extract called carmine, which is a dye made from chemically processed cochineal.

Facts about cochineal:
1. It takes between 70,000–100,000 bugs to make 1kg of dye.
2. France is the world's biggest importer of cochineal.
3. Cochineal currently costs $60–80 per kilo.
4. You might think cochineal is a little weird. I think it's quite beautiful.

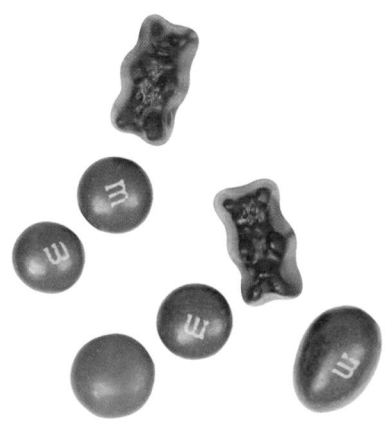

2

DIPPING AND SPREADING

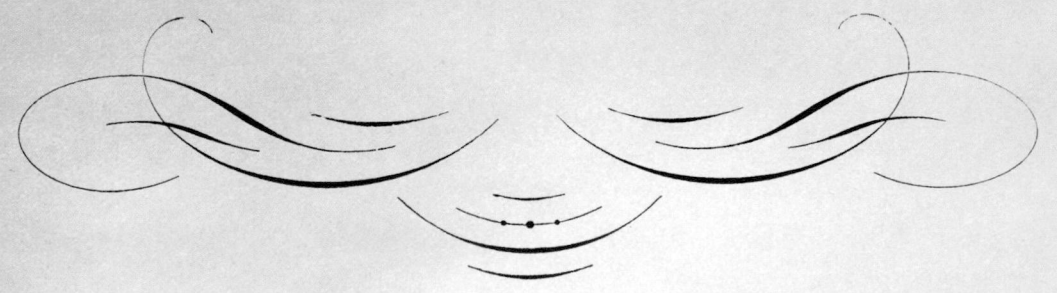

I HAVE ONE SMALL REQUEST: please, please, please get your friends to make their own butter. While the dishes in this chapter are all fun, delicious, hands-on, shareable numbers that get people interacting with their food (even if it's just by spreading something delicious on their bread), I can't tell you how extraordinary the simple task of DIY butter churning can be. There's something magical about this little act of creation that means your friends will never forget the experience – which is what we're up to here after all. Kids absolutely love making their own butter, but adults are invariably reduced to wide-eyed, childish delight by it too.

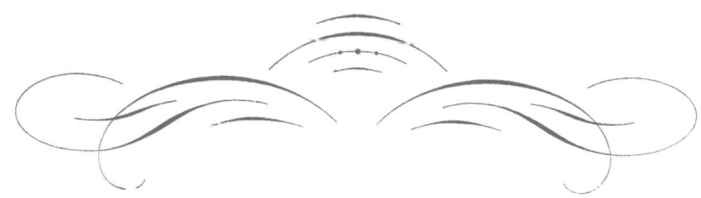

DO-IT-YOURSELF BUTTER WITH BREAD

There's a lovely sense of discovery in making your own butter, especially when you then spread it on bread and eat it immediately. I can't recommend this recipe enough: it's dead easy to do, and it's loads of fun.

Butter is simply cream or milk that has been churned until the watery buttermilk separates from the butterfat, and this is easily done by pouring some room-temperature double cream into a jam jar and shaking it for a few minutes. The buttery fat coagulates into a handsome lump in the middle of a pool of watery buttermilk. The buttermilk is drained away, and the remaining butter is ready for use. It tastes a little creamier than normal butter because you won't be able to extract quite as much buttermilk as the dairy can, but it's still delicious. If the cream is cold from the fridge it will still work but it'll take a lot longer (10–15 minutes) and it'll go through a disheartening whipped-cream stage that you feel may never end!

The science of the whole affair is fascinating, and there are few better explanations of it than the brilliant Harold McGee in *On Food and Cooking*, should you fancy taking a look. He quotes Seamus Heaney's description of butter as 'coagulated sunlight'.

SERVES 6

900ml double cream,
    at room temperature
6 medium-sized jam jars, very clean
fresh crusty bread and salt, to serve

Give everyone an empty jam jar and get them to add double cream until each jar is one third full, then replace the lid. Tell your friends to shake their jars until the butter solids have separated from the buttermilk, which should take about 2–4 minutes. You can tell when it's ready because you'll feel it thumping as you shake your jar.

When the butter has been churned to satisfaction, place a bowl in the middle of the table with a sieve sitting in it, lined with a clean tea-towel or piece of muslin. Get your friends to pour the contents of their jam jars onto the tea-towel, and leave to drain for one minute. After the watery buttermilk has drained away, you'll be left with butter. Take the tea towel by each of the four edges and bring them together over the bowl. Twist and squeeze to wring out any excess buttermilk.

Serve the freshly churned butter straight away with some crusty bread – homemade would obviously be a joy – and some salt, for those who prefer salty butter.

Homemade butter will keep in the fridge for a week or so. It's good for cooking but not for frying as the slightly higher water content may make it spit and burn in a frying pan.

FLOWERPOT-BAKED BREAD

Terracotta flowerpots have been fired at very high temperatures in a kiln, so they can cope with being baked again to make little breads, and they also help to create a great crust. You can use pretty much any bread recipe for this – I've given you a basic white bread version but you can try fruit ones, cheesy ones or muffins.

If you want a shortcut to making your own bread dough (it does take a little application after all) and you own a breadmaking machine, you should be able to get it to do the whole dough-making process and stop before the baking bit. Then you just transfer the dough really carefully (so that you don't knock the air out of the dough) into the flowerpots and bake.

By the way, it's impossible to tell you how many flowerpot loaves this recipe makes – it all depends on the size of your pots! Ensure that they are unglazed and new or at least very clean.

MAKES ABOUT 800G

1 sachet easy-blend yeast
2 teaspoons sugar
500g strong white flour
    (plus extra for kneading)
1 tablespoon salt
butter, for greasing

Put the yeast and sugar in a cup with a tablespoon of warm water and stir until dissolved. In a large bowl, stir together the flour, salt and the dissolved yeast and sugar.

Measure 300ml warm water into a jug and slowly add it to the flour mixture, stirring continuously with a wooden spoon. Continue to add the water, a splash at a time, until you have a nice moist dough. (The exact amount of water required will depend on the type of flour you're using.)

Tip the dough out onto a large floured surface and start kneading it with your hands. (You'll find it easier if you cover your hands with flour before you start.) Push down and away at the dough with the heel of your palms, then roll and fold the dough. You'll need to push, shove and manhandle the dough for a good 5 minutes until it's smooth and elastic. Add more water if the dough feels dry and more flour if it feels too sticky.

Lightly oil a large bowl and place the dough in it, then cover this with clingfilm and leave it somewhere warm for about an hour to prove and rise. After an hour it should have doubled in size.

If your flowerpots have large holes in the bottom, slip a piece of foil over them. Grease the insides of the pots really, really well, using lots of butter, then sprinkle a little flour over the butter.

Tip the dough out onto a floured surface and knock it back (this reduces the size of it again) by kneading it for a further minute. Then divide it up between your flowerpots so that the dough half-fills each one. Sprinkle a little flour over the dough in each pot. Cover the pots with a tea-towel and leave the dough to rise again for a further 45 minutes. Meanwhile, preheat the oven to 200°C.

Bake your bread in the oven. Small pots will need about 15–30 minutes, larger ones 30–45 minutes. You'll need to keep an eye on them as the cooking time will depend on the size of your pots. When the loaves are golden brown on top, remove them from the oven and leave on cooling racks to cool for 10 minutes or so before serving – in the flowerpots, of course.

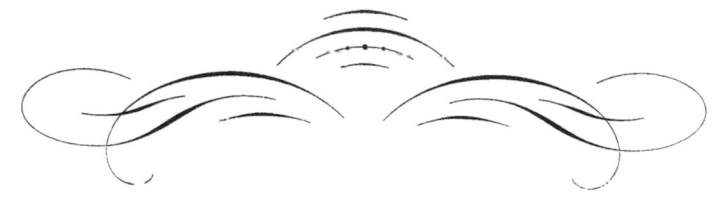

DIY BRUSCHETTA

The original idea behind these wildly popular Tuscan snacks was to show off the new season's olive oil harvest. Slices of hot toast were rubbed with garlic before being drenched in oil and sprinkled with salt. It's certainly a good way to make the flavours of olive oil sing, much like boiling new potatoes and pouring oil and salt over them while they're still steaming hot. (I'm terrible for nicking them straight out of the pot before anyone else can get their hands on them.)

I love serving unmade bruschetta by putting all the ingredients on the table and letting everyone build their own. My friends can then play with the flavours they love best and it's fun to share ideas and to steal a nibble from the person sitting next to you. As with pizzas, you'll often find that less is more: resist the temptation to combine loads of ingredients, as you'll tend to drown flavours out. The classic combination is ripe tomatoes and basil leaves.

bread slices, preferably sourdough or ciabatta (grilled on a
    ridged grill if you have one)
raw garlic cloves, halved, for rubbing on the bread
extra virgin olive oil
sea salt flakes

TOPPING SUGGESTIONS
- ripe tomatoes, roughly chopped and drained in a colander
- fresh basil leaves
- pitted olives
- mozzarella, torn into large pieces
- rocket leaves
- prosciutto (thinly-sliced dry-cured Italian ham)
- asparagus spears, blanched
- anchovies in oil
- balsamic vinegar
- Parmesan (with a potato peeler for shaving)
- roasted whole garlic cloves (see right)
- tomato salsa (see right)
- grilled aubergines, courgettes and/or peppers (see right)

Cut the bread into small slices and then grill them (on a ridged grill pan if you have one). Rub each slice with half a clove of raw garlic and then put the toasts on the table.

Choose a selection from the ingredients above and recipes (see right) – tomatoes and fresh basil leaves are must-haves – then serve them in bowls or plates. Encourage your guests to dive in, splash a large slug of olive oil over their bruschetta, sprinkle with salt, then choose from the variety of toppings.

ROASTED WHOLE GARLIC CLOVES

These make a wonderful bruschetta ingredient, but you can also keep them in the fridge to use as a pasta sauce, or for adding sparkle and wonder to gravies and stews etc. After the garlic has been roasted, you just squeeze a clove and a slug of sweet, mild garlic paste will pop out of the end. This is great to spread straight onto the bruschetta.

whole garlic heads
extra-virgin olive oil
salt and pepper
fresh thyme leaves (optional)

Preheat the oven to 180°C. Pull the papery outer skins off a head of garlic to allow access to the cloves. Place the head of garlic onto a piece of aluminium foil about 14cm square, then pour a slug of olive oil into the middle so that it seeps into the head. Sprinkle with salt and pepper and a few thyme leaves (if you have any). Pull up the corners of the foil and scrunch it into a pear shape. Roast for about an hour. Leave to cool a little before serving.

GRILLED AUBERGINES AND COURGETTES

Slice aubergines and courgettes to the thickness of a pound coin, then toss in olive oil, salt and pepper. Grill them on a ridged grill pan until nicely browned.

Make more than you need, then you can use them later for salads or couscous.

TOMATO SALSA

500g ripe, full-flavoured tomatoes
150g olives, roughly chopped
1 garlic clove, crushed
a handful of shredded basil leaves
balsamic vinegar
salt and pepper
extra virgin olive oil

Roughly chop the tomatoes (no need to peel them), then leave in a colander for 10 minutes to drain away some of the juices and pips. Put them in a bowl and stir in the chopped olives, crushed garlic, shredded basil leaves, a slug of balsamic vinegar, salt and pepper and plenty of extra-virgin olive oil.

GRILLED PEPPERS

If you've ever wondered why grilled red peppers are so expensive in the delicatessen, I can confirm that it's because they are pretty fiddly to prepare. I love doing this, but only when I'm not too pushed for time!

Cook whole peppers under a high grill, turning every 10 minutes until the skins are blackened all over. Wrap them in a plastic bag and leave to sweat for 15 minutes or so, then halve them, scrape the seeds out of the insides and remove the skins with a flat knife. Save all the ugly but sweet, flavour-packed juices and mix them together with the peppers in a bowl.

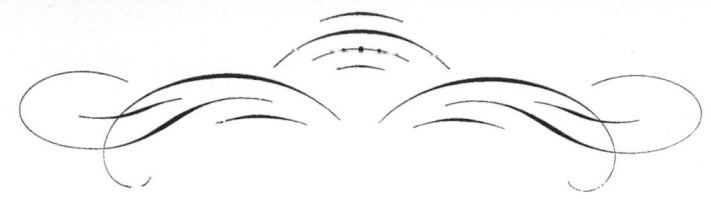

WHOLE BAKED VACHERIN CHEESE

This is an easy way to turn supper into a celebration. Vacherin is a raw cow's milk cheese that's wrapped in a thin band of spruce, and then packed in a circular wooden box. The packaging, and the fact that this superb cheese has a natural velvety crust concealing its creamy body, makes it perfect for baking into an extraordinarily easy and unctuous fondue. The best Vacherin arrives in my local cheese shop in late autumn, so we eat this as a way of cheering and warming everyone up at the onset of winter.

SERVES 4 AS A MAIN COURSE

500g boxed Vacherin cheese,
    ripe and ready
50ml white wine (a fruity
    Gewürztraminer is fabulous for this)

FOR DIPPING
steamed baby new potatoes
chunks of crusty bread
blanched green beans
slices of good cured ham,
    preferably Serrano
pickled gherkins

Preheat the oven to 180°C. Take the lid off the cheese, then wrap the sides and bottom of the box in foil without covering the top of the cheese. Poke a few holes in the crust with a fork, then pour the white wine over the top. Replace the lid so it sits loosely on top. Bake in the oven for 25 minutes.

Take the lid off the box then slice off the crust (reserve it for munching though). Place the box in the middle of the table, surrounded by the potatoes, bread, beans, ham and pickled gherkins. Encourage everyone to serve themselves by skewering a selection of ingredients to dip into the melted cheese.

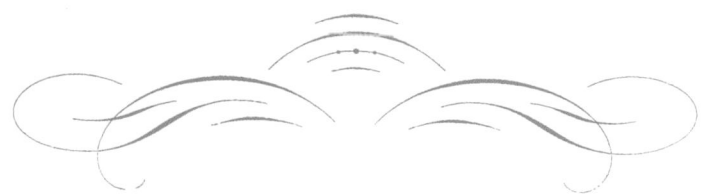

HEAD CHEESE: THE EASY VERSION

Sounds bizarre, I know, but 'head cheese' is just an old name for brawn – a sort of pâté made from a pig's head. The French still call it *fromage de tête*, and you can buy veal or pig's fromage in most French markets. It is best cut into slices and eaten with pickled gherkins, mustard and bread.

You can make an easy version of this or, if you fancy, you can make an absurdly complicated one. In my first book, *Gastronaut*, I indulged myself so much that I stretched the recipe out to eight pages. (It's the only recipe in the world that starts with the phrase 'I'm rarely at home to Mr Existential Angst, but…'), but the book you now hold in your hands is a practical cookbook, so here's the easy version. The recipe is still something of a project, as you need to brine the meat for a day first and you need to get up close and personal to a pig's head, which, if you've never done it before, is quite an experience. That said there's nothing difficult here, it's an absurdly cheap dish, it's delicious, and in my view any usable part of a pig that ends up getting thrown away is a terrible waste.

Three hints: firstly, deal with your pig's head as soon as you've got it home – many fridges are too small to accommodate one, and they go off quickly at room temperature. Secondly, don't forget that you'll need a pan large enough to contain the pig's head and more. Thirdly, leave the window open when you boil the head otherwise the whole house will smell of pâté!

1kg salt
1 pig's head, ears removed and
    reserved (ask the butcher to do this if you'd rather)
2 pig's trotters (optional)
2 onions, peeled but kept whole
4 bay leaves
10 peppercorns
2 cloves (no more!)
1 teaspoon coriander seeds
a small handful of thyme
a large handful of chopped parsley
juice of ½ lemon

First clean your pig's head. Remove any hairs, either using a razor or by burning them off with a blowtorch, and don't forget to clean the ears and around the snout thoroughly too. Put the salt and 1 litre of water into a big pan (large enough to fit the pig's head with room to spare). Heat gently, stirring until the salt dissolves. Then remove the pan from the heat, add the head, ears and trotters and pour over enough cold water to completely cover the head. Cover the pan with a lid and place somewhere cool for 24 hours.

Remove and rinse the head, ears and trotters, then drain and rinse the pan and replace the meat. Add the onions, bay leaves, peppercorns, cloves, coriander seeds and thyme and cover with cold water. Bring to the boil, skim any scum from the surface and reduce to a gentle simmer. Cook uncovered for about 4 hours, topping up the water if the level drops to reveal the head. After 4 hours the meat should be so tender that it falls off the bones easily.

Remove the meat from the cooking broth (reserving the broth) and leave until cool enough to handle. Now for the icky bit. Pull all the skin, meat and fat off the head and ears and reserve. Pull the tongue out, peel off and discard the outer skin and add the tongue to the rest of the meat. Now do the same with the trotters, reserving the lovely unctuous bits, but rejecting any harder skin.

Chop the meat roughly and place in a bowl. Stir in the parsley and lemon juice and add a strained ladleful of the cooking broth to moisten it. Line a dish or two (a terrine dish would be great) with clingfilm and add the head cheese mixture. Put a weight on top to compress it and squeeze out air, and refrigerate overnight to set. The head cheese will keep in the fridge for up to 2 weeks. Eat like pâté or fry it and serve with potatoes, Puy lentils and salad.

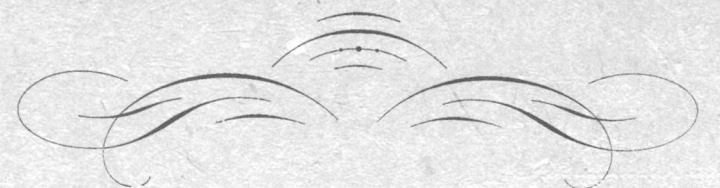

A LITTLE SELECTION OF FONDUES

Let's face it, fondues have had a bad press. At some point in the seventies they got bundled together with the dropping of keys into bowls and – worse – sloppy ratatouille served as though it's the height of sophistication. But if you've got a fondue set at home gathering dust, nip to the hardware store for a bottle of paraffin fuel and try one of these recipes (or indeed, the recipes for Bagna Càuda, Shabu-shabu or Toffee Fondue, see pages 53, 128 and 202 respectively). Don't worry if you don't have fondue skewers – forks should do fine. If you have any fondue left over, don't throw it away – I use it as a fantastic sauce to go with fish or as a topping for baked potatoes, and it keeps surprisingly well in the fridge.

SPINACH FONDUE

SERVES 6

1.5kg spinach, thickest stalks pulled off
3 garlic cloves, peeled and finely chopped
large knob of butter
220ml cider
450g mature Cheddar cheese, grated
salt and freshly ground black pepper
2 pinches of nutmeg

TO SERVE
small potatoes, steamed or boiled
carrots, cut into sticks and blanched
cauliflower florets, blanched
broccoli florets, blanched
endive leaves, separated
radishes
1 large baguette, cut into bite-sized cubes

Wash the spinach, give it a good shake and put it into a large saucepan with the garlic, salt and pepper. Place the pan over a low heat and cook for about 6–8 minutes, stirring occasionally, until the spinach has wilted. Drain in a colander, pressing well to strain off the water (you need to get it really dry so the fondue isn't watery). Place in a food-processor with a knob of butter and purée until smooth.

Bring the cider to a simmer in a fondue pan or thick-based saucepan. Reduce the heat, then mix in the cheese, stirring gently as it melts. Add the nutmeg and spinach, season and stir to mix. Add a little more cider if it feels too stiff.

You can prepare your dipping vegetables at this stage (see above), as the fondue will happily sit for a while, and it reheats very easily without the texture spoiling.

Place the pan of fondue onto a fondue warmer or camping stove on the table and keep warm, but try not to boil. Serve with the vegetables and bread cubes to dip into it.

CHEDDAR AND CIDER FONDUE

SERVES 6

200ml strong cider
350g mature Cheddar cheese, grated
1 tablespoon cornflour, mixed into a
    paste with a few splashes of cold water
1 teaspoon English mustard
splash of Worcester sauce
freshly ground black pepper

TO SERVE
3 apples
juice of ½ lemon or lime
1 large baguette
small potatoes, steamed or boiled
carrots, cut into sticks and blanched
cauliflower florets, blanched
broccoli florets, blanched
radishes

Bring the cider to a simmer in a fondue pan or thick-based saucepan. Reduce the heat, then mix in the grated cheese, cornflour paste and mustard. Stir gently until all the cheese has melted and it becomes a good sticky goo. Add the Worcester sauce to taste, then test the consistency by dipping a piece of bread into the fondue. Add more cider to water it down or more cheese to make it firmer as you see fit. Reduce the heat so that it doesn't boil, but keep warm until you're ready to eat.

Peel and core the apples, chop them into bite-sized pieces then toss them in the lemon or lime juice to stop them going brown. Chop the baguette into thumb-sized pieces.

Place the pan of molten cheese onto a fondue warmer or camping stove and keep warm, but try not to let it boil. Serve with the prepared vegetables, fruit and bread for dipping.

CRAB FONDUE

SERVES 6

250g cream cheese
125g Caerphilly or Cheddar cheese, grated
250g crab meat (brown and white)
50ml white wine
juice of 1 lemon
a handful of fresh dill or parsley,
    finely chopped
splash of Tabasco
splash of Worcester sauce

TO SERVE
2 apples
juice of ½ lemon or lime
1 large baguette
radishes
asparagus spears, blanched
cucumber, cut into sticks
carrot, cut into sticks, blanched
broccoli florets, blanched

Combine all the fondue ingredients in a fondue pan or thick-based saucepan and put over a low heat. Stir as the cheese melts until all the ingredients are well mixed. Check the Tabasco levels (it should have a definite tang of chilli heat) and adjust if necessary.

Peel and core the apples, chop them into bite-sized pieces then toss them in the lemon or lime juice to stop them going brown. Chop the baguette into thumb-sized pieces.

Place the pan of crab and cheese onto a fondue warmer or camping stove to keep warm (but not hot or boiling). Serve the fondue with the prepared vegetables, fruit and bread to dip in.

BAGNA CÀUDA

Roughly translated as 'hot bath', *bagna càuda* is basically an Italian version of crudités: instead of dipping your vegetables into delicate mayonnaise, you sink them into a piquant bath of garlicky, oily, anchovy stuff that has such a gutsy taste, it smacks of the primordial soup of life itself.

This provides all the wonderful communal experience of the cheese fondue without the... well... the cheesiness. Unlike a cheese fondue, where you're essentially using bread to hoof out as much viscous matter as you can, only a thin coating of the 'hot bath' is needed to provide all the necessary flavour. That said, it's a much runnier substance, so you can't really dip your vegetable into a saucepan in the middle of the table, otherwise it drips everywhere! Much better to give everyone a bowl of their own, so that they can serve themselves the bagna càuda a ladle at a time and grab vegetables as they fancy.

SERVES 6

FOR THE BAGNA CÀUDA
300ml milk
12 fat garlic cloves, peeled
25–30 tinned anchovies in oil, oil
    reserved (this is about 3 small
    50g tins of anchovies. If you can
    only find salted anchovies, rinse
    them first)
150g butter, diced
150ml extra virgin olive oil
150ml double cream

FOR DIPPING, A SELECTION OF
THE FOLLOWING:
small potatoes, steamed or boiled
radishes
celery, cut into large strips
asparagus, blanched
radicchio or endive
sweet potato, cut into long chips and
    roasted until lightly browned
baby carrots, blanched
red and yellow peppers, cut into long,
    thick slices
small baby artichokes, halved
crusty bread

To make the bagna càuda, pour the milk into a small thick-based saucepan, add the garlic cloves and heat the pan until the millk reaches a gentle simmer. (If you want a really garlicky sauce, crush the garlic into the milk and skip this simmering.) Cover the pan and simmer the milk gently for 8–12 minutes until you can easily crush the garlic cloves into the milk using the back of a fork.

Add the anchovies to the garlic and milk and cook for a further 5 minutes until they disintegrate. Add the butter, olive oil and reserved oil from the tinned anchovies and stir until the butter starts to foam a little. Add the cream and heat until simmering then remove the pan from the heat and gently whisk the sauce into a runny paste.

Arrange the vegetables on a large serving platter in the centre of the table, give everyone a small bowl, and put the saucepan of bagna càuda straight onto the table (don't forget to put a heat-resistant mat down first), with a ladle so that your friends can serve themselves.

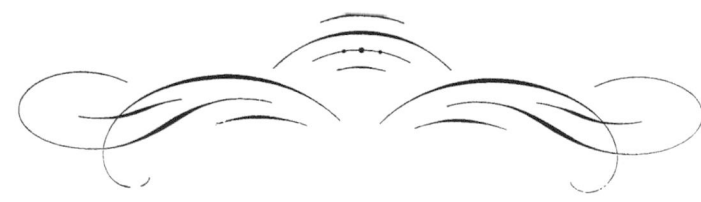

OUTRAGEOUSLY RICH CHICKEN LIVER PARFAIT

This is velvety smooth, rich, luxurious to the tongue and strangely refined for something so cheap and simple to cook. I've tested lots of painfully complex parfait recipes, but they're so time-consuming to make that I've spent a fair amount of time over the last ten years refining this one to achieve maximum unctuation from minimum faff. (By the way, don't try using whisky instead of brandy, even if you're desperate. I know from bitter experience that it makes the parfait disgusting!)

MAKES 500G, ENOUGH TO SERVE 10 AS A STARTER

250g free-range chicken livers
250g butter, preferably unsalted
1 cinnamon stick
pinch of freshly grated nutmeg
2 garlic cloves, crushed
2 fresh thyme sprigs
2 tablespoons brandy (or Calvados
    for a nice twist)
1 teaspoon salt
1 teaspoon fresh thyme leaves
crusty bread to serve

First prepare the chicken livers. Pull off and discard any stringy bits, fat, and dark- or greenish-looking scraps, and gently cut or pull out any of the larger blood vessels that will easily come away.

Melt the butter in a thick-based frying pan until gently bubbling, then add the cinnamon, nutmeg, garlic and chicken livers and cook over a low heat for about 6–10 minutes, turning the livers once. Check them after 6 minutes: they should still be just pink in the middle, and not grey. Using tongs, remove the livers from the pan to the bowl of a food-processor.

Add the thyme sprigs to the pan and put it back on a low heat. Carefully add the brandy or Calvados and let it bubble away for about 4 minutes, or until the alcohol smell has gone, leaving just the brandy flavours. (If you're experienced in flambéing, turn the extractor fan off, turn the heat up to high and carefully burn off the alcohol for 30 seconds.)

Remove the pan from the heat, discard the cinnamon stick and thyme sprigs, then carefully pour the contents of the pan into the food-processor. Season with the salt and blend for 4 minutes, or until smooth and creamy. Pour the mixture into small bowls, coffee cups or teacups for individual servings (or a large jar), scatter a few thyme leaves on top and refrigerate for at least an hour until solid.

Serve with crusty bread and a good glass of hefty red wine.

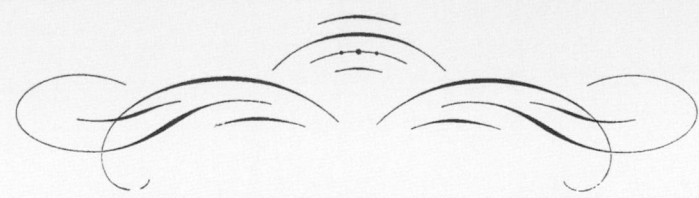

BONE MARROW ON TOAST

Bone marrow, championed by Fergus Henderson at his legendary St John restaurant in London, home of great offal, is the very definition of unctuousness. I always keep veal bones in the freezer so that I can add them to stews for extra deliciousness and stickiness, and every now and then I can't resist roasting them and spreading the marrow on some good sourdough toast.

SERVES 6

12 fat pieces of veal bone,
   each about 6–7cm long

TO SERVE
sourdough toast
lemon wedges
finely chopped parsley
flaky salt crystals

Preheat your oven to 180°C. Place the bones upright in a roasting tray and roast them for about 15 minutes until the marrow inside is soft, shrinking a little from the bone around it, but has a light crust on top. Don't cook them for too long or the marrow will begin to melt away.

Serve the whole bones with the toast, lemon wedges, parsley and salt. You'll need to offer teaspoons for your friends to use to dig the marrow out (the handle of the spoon often comes in handy), spreading it onto their toast and adding a squirt of lemon juice and a sprinkling of parsley and salt to taste.

3

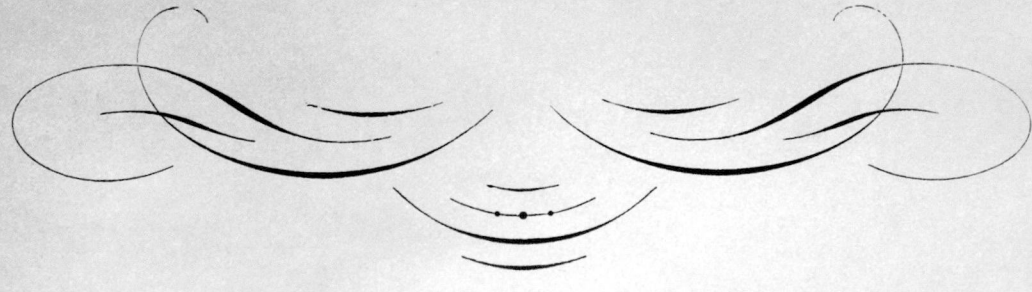

SOUPS

SOUPS ARE USUALLY THOUGHT OF AS homely, life-enhancing comfort foods rather than extraordinary flights of fancy. Well, it's time to turn these preconceptions on their heads with a few of my favourite spectacular liquid dishes. Of course, even the simple chilled soup can be turned into a journey of discovery if you serve it in an ice bowl or a pumpkin cauldron. But it's also great fun to serve people unusual food like nettles – if your friends have never eaten them before they add a wonderful sense of drama and suspense to dinner, and if they have eaten them before, you can revel in the fact that they don't tingle your tongue, and instead they are both delicious and free. My only word of advice is that you keep the Windbreaker Soup away from any easily-offended (or explosively flatulent) aged relatives.

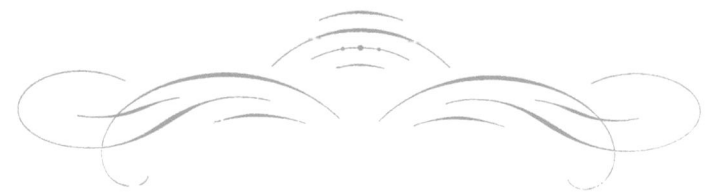

AVOCADO AND LIME SOUP IN AN ICE BOWL

Are ice bowls a celebration or an affectation? It's all in the delivery really. If you're comfortable in your skin and you love going to town to give your friends a night they'll never forget, go for it.

It's a pretty simple process: basically, you pour some water into a large bowl then place another bowl into it with a weight on top, then freeze. You'll need to make your ice bowl at least a day before you need it. The ice needs to set overnight, and it's just too stressful to make it on the day.

If you want something really spectacular, use distilled water, which tends not to cloud when frozen. You can add pretty much anything to the ice to decorate it: I've used everything from flower petals to Cadbury's Creme Eggs. For the one in the photo I raided my daughters' toy box.

I'm a big fan of cold soups in the summer, and I love this zesty, shocking-green avocado and lime number, which reminds me of an exhilarating trip to Mexico. You need good ripe avocados for this.

SERVES 4

4 ripe avocados, peeled and stoned
2 garlic cloves, chopped, then mashed
    with ½ teaspoon salt
zest and juice of 2 limes
1 green chilli, deseeded and finely chopped
1 litre vegetable or light chicken stock
2 handfuls of coriander leaves and stalks

Place the avocados, mashed garlic, lime zest and juice, chilli, half of the stock and all except a few sprigs of the chopped coriander in a food processor and blitz until smooth. Pour into a large bowl and add the rest of the stock then stir together.

Lay a piece of clingfilm on the surface of the soup to prevent it turning brown, then chill for 1–2 hours. To serve, pour into the ice bowl (if you've made one) and scatter the remaining coriander on top.

TO MAKE THE ICE BOWL YOU WILL NEED:
1 large Pyrex or freezerproof bowl
    (this will need to fit in your freezer
    and will be the outer size of your
    ice bowl)
1 smaller Pyrex or freezerproof bowl
    (this will be the inner size of your
    serving bowl)
decorations – toy figures, flowers or
    flower petals (optional)
water, distilled if possible

In the larger bowl, spread a layer of your decorations on the base and a little way up the sides. Put the smaller bowl on top to hold them there, then squeeze the rest into the gap between the bowls (NB: this gap should be at least 2cm thick). Put something heavy into the smaller bowl to hold it down, then pour water into the gap until it's full. Place in the freezer overnight.

Just before you're ready to use it, remove the bowl from the freezer, place in a sink of lukewarm water and pour some lukewarm water into the inner bowl so that the ice bowl warms up and you can gently slip it out. Remember to place the bowl on a tray, as it will begin to melt, particularly if you're serving the soup outdoors in the sunshine.

IF YOU'RE USING FLOWERS OR SMALL DECORATIONS:
Put the larger bowl in the sink and quarter fill with water. Add decorations, then float the smaller bowl on top. Place a small chopping board on top and push the smaller bowl down, until the chopping board lays flat on the surface, making sure that the inner bowl is right in the middle of the larger one. Check the decorations, then weight the board down with something heavy. Spill a little more water from the bowl (to make it easier to carry), then place in the freezer overnight.

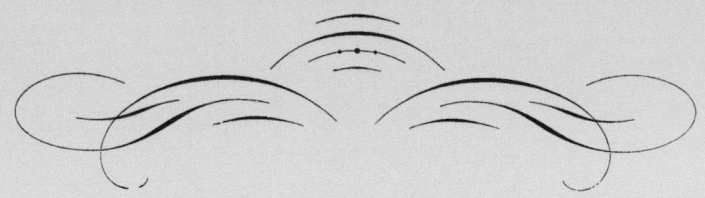

BLOODY MARY SOUP

I enjoy a Bloody Mary most when it's served on the bar semi-prepared and accompanied by its little team of helpers: a bottle of Tabasco sauce, another of Worcester sauce, a little shaker of celery salt and a celery-stick stirrer. Such old-fashioned serving is rare these days, which is a shame, as I like to have control over my flavours, and offering guests a choice would seem like the decent thing to do when you consider that in the chilli-heat department, one man's tongue-tickler is another man's Ring of Fire.

This rich and fiery soup is on a different planet from regular tomato ones, and allows your friends to decide how hot they want it by providing the base soup but leaving the key flavouring ingredients on the table for them to add at will. If you wish, you can substitute the roasted tomatoes with tins of chopped plum tomatoes heated up with a tablespoon of sugar and perhaps some extra tomato purée, but the recipe below gives a wonderfully intense flavour.

SERVES 6

2kg ripe full-flavoured tomatoes
3 tablespoons extra virgin olive oil
2 teaspoons caster sugar
salt and pepper
1 tablespoon sherry (or
    balsamic) vinegar
500ml vegetable stock, warmed

TO SERVE
6 celery stalks
horseradish sauce
6 tablespoons vodka, (in individual shot
    glasses, if you'd prefer)
a small jug of dry sherry
Tabasco sauce
Worcester sauce
salt and freshly ground black pepper
1 lemon, cut into 6 segments

Preheat the oven to 200°C. Halve the tomatoes and cut out the cores then place them in a roasting tin with the olive oil, sugar and salt and pepper. Toss them around to coat, then roast for about 30 minutes, or until they begin to brown.

Put the roasted tomatoes in a blender with the vinegar and blitz them until smooth, adding a little of the stock if needed. Heat the stock in a pan, then add the puréed tomatoes and heat until simmering.

Serve the tomato soup in bowls, with a celery stalk in each. Place the rest of the ingredients on the table for your friends to create the flavourings they desire.

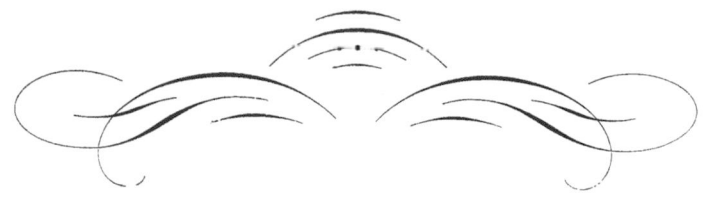

NETTLE SOUP

There's always a little frisson of fear when you put the first spoonful of nettle soup to your lips, no matter how many times you may have tried it. The sting is, of course, neutralised by boiling the nettles – though it's always more fun not to tell your friends and family this.

I think that nettle soup tastes a little like liquid grass – in a good way. It certainly has an uplifting effect, mainly because I only eat it in spring, just as summer is becoming a possibility once more. Be careful if you make this any later in the year; I've had several batches ruined by the bitterness of more mature nettles. You're really looking for new shoots that are only a few inches high. Make sure you collect them from an area that's unpolluted and unsprayed. Oh, and remember to wear gloves!

SERVES 4

a large carrier bag, packed with freshly
    picked, new-growth spring nettles
50g butter
1 large onion, finely chopped
200g peeled potatoes, roughly chopped

1 litre light vegetable or chicken stock
    (a good bouillon or cube stock would be fine)
salt and freshly ground black pepper
200ml crème fraîche
fresh crusty bread and butter, to serve

Pick through the nettles and discard thick stalks, stems, flowers and bugs. Wash the nettles thoroughly in cold water, then put in a colander to drain. Melt the butter in a saucepan, add the onion and cook over a low heat until soft and golden. Add the potatoes and nettles and cook for a further 10 minutes. Add the stock and bring to a boil, then reduce the heat and simmer gently for 15 minutes. Whizz the soup in a blender then add salt and pepper to taste. Divide the soup between four warmed bowls, add a dollop of crème fraîche to each and serve with bread and butter.

MELON, LIME AND MINT SOUP

A perfect starter for a hot, sunny day: a cold soup served in the husk of the melon.

SERVES 6

3 ripe melons, chilled
    (Galia or Cantaloupe are great)
200ml orange juice
zest and juice of 1 lime
pinch of salt
1 teaspoon sugar
a handful of fresh mint leaves

Cut the melons in half, scoop out the pips and discard. Shave a very thin slice from the underside of each melon bowl so that it will stand up firmly. Scoop the flesh out of

the melons, leaving behind just enough for the bowl to stand (and being careful not to pierce the bottom).

Put all the melon flesh into a food-processor with the orange juice, lime juice, salt, sugar and half of the mint leaves and whizz until smooth. If the mixture is too stiff, add a little more orange juice. Pour into the melon bowls.

If you kept the melons in the fridge you can serve the soup straight away. If not, refrigerate for about 30 minutes. Scatter the lime zest and remaining mint leaves on top just before serving.

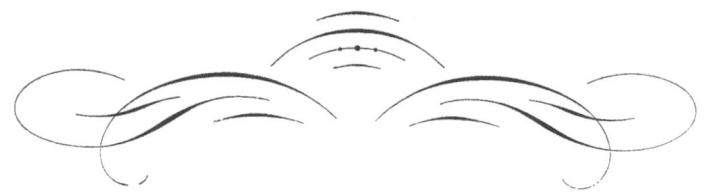

JERUSALEM ARTICHOKE 'WINDBREAKER' SOUP

Jerusalem artichokes make a delicious soup and have a deep sweetness similar to globe artichokes, despite being entirely unrelated to them. But there are other, fruitier reasons for the inclusion of these vegetables in an extraordinary cookbook. Jerusalem artichokes are rampant little buggers on two fronts. Firstly, I can't get rid of them from my allotment, no matter how hard I try. I planted them about five years ago, and very abundant they are too, despite the poor soil. But after producing way more artichokes than we could eat or even give away, I tried to pull them out, but without success. Consequently, this may well be the most thoroughly tested recipe in the book.

Secondly, and more amusingly, Jerusalem artichokes are rampant when they're inside you, creating a quite astonishing amount of wind. It's thought to be due to inulin, a sugar that's hard to digest in your smaller intestine, but which the flora in your larger intestine go bonkers for, breaking down with a whoop and a holler and producing lots and lots of gas in the process. You could see this as a disadvantage, of course, but wind really is an essential part of our digestion (if you didn't fart you'd explode), and Jerusalem artichokes are a practical and dynamic way of explaining the workings of the digestive system, especially to kids, who love the effects. By the way, it may take a little while for the inulin to do its job – possibly not until your friends have gone home, which may be a blessing, depending on your point of view, and your love of *schadenfreude*.

SERVES 6

100g butter
1 large onion, finely chopped
100g carrots, peeled and
   roughly chopped
100g celery (or celeriac),
   roughly chopped
750g Jerusalem artichokes, scrubbed
   clean (tough-skinned varieties should
   be peeled) and roughly chopped
1.5 litres chicken or vegetable stock (a
   good bouillon or cube stock would do)
salt and freshly ground black pepper
200g crème fraîche

Melt the butter in a large heavy-based saucepan, then add the onion, carrots, celery and artichokes and cook over a medium heat for 15 minutes, stirring frequently.

Add the stock, bring to the boil, then reduce the heat and simmer for another 15 minutes. Transfer to a food-processor and whizz in batches until smooth. Season with salt and pepper to taste, then pour the soup into warmed bowls, add a dollop of crème fraîche to each one and serve.

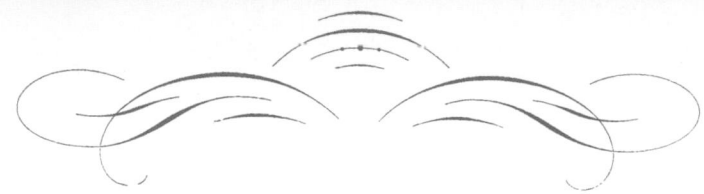

FRAGRANT PUMPKIN THAI NOODLE SOUP

This really is a fabulous use of a remarkable vegetable. The pumpkin's tough skin keeps the precious flesh inside fresh from the end of summer right through until spring, if stored in a cool, dry place, and that golden flesh yields a surprising depth of flavour and sweetness, especially when roasted, which makes it a great replacement for meat in pasta sauces.

One pumpkin yields so much flesh to eat that I thought it only fair to supply four recipes instead of just the one. You start by making this soul-meltingly delicious Thai soup, which you can serve in the hollowed-out pumpkin 'cauldron'. The next day you can cut the remaining pumpkin into pieces for roasting, and use it as a great accompaniment for a Sunday roast, in a salad or a rich pasta sauce (see recipes over the page).

SERVES 4

1 large pumpkin, weighing at least 4kg
    (or, if you don't want to serve the soup in
    a cauldron and use the remaining flesh for
    other recipes, 600g pumpkin flesh)
1 large bunch of fresh coriander, stalks
    finely chopped and leaves roughly chopped
4 fat garlic cloves, peeled and roughly chopped
6cm piece of ginger, peeled and grated
½ red chilli, finely chopped
2 tablespoons sesame oil
1 tablespoon vegetable oil
2 teaspoons Thai fish sauce (nam pla)
1 teaspoon ground cumin
3 lemongrass stalks, outer leaves
    removed, finely chopped
6 kaffir lime leaves (optional)
400ml tin coconut milk
1 litre fish stock (or chicken or vegetable
    stock – stock cubes would be fine)
zest and juice of 1 lime
200g dried egg noodles

Cut the top quarter off the pumpkin to make a large circular lid (you'll use the flesh from this to make the soup). Scrape out the seeds and stringy parts from both parts of the pumpkin and discard them. Set the main piece aside (but do not refrigerate).

Cut some (but not all) of the flesh from inside the lid – you'll need about 600g – then cut it into small (2cm) square chunks. Leave enough of the flesh on the pumpkin that it won't collapse when used as a bowl (use the rest for the next recipes).

Put the coriander stalks (reserve the leaves for garnishing), garlic, ginger, chilli, sesame oil, vegetable oil, Thai fish sauce, cumin, lemongrass and lime leaves (if using) into a bowl or mortar and whizz using a small hand blender or crush with a pestle until you have a paste.

Put a large heavy-based saucepan on a low heat and very gently fry the herb and spice mixture for 5 minutes. Add the coconut milk and stock to the saucepan and stir to combine, then add the pumpkin chunks. Bring to the boil then reduce the heat and simmer gently for about 15 minutes until the pumpkin is tender.

Add the lime zest and juice and the egg noodles and cook for a further 4 minutes, or until the noodles are cooked. Pour the hot soup into the pumpkin cauldron and place on the table for serving. After use, rinse out the pumpkin cauldron and keep cool to use the flesh for the following recipes next day.

3 MORE USES FOR YOUR PUMPKIN

ROASTED PUMPKIN

1kg pumpkin flesh, cut into thick slices
3 tablespoons olive oil
2 teaspoons coriander seeds, roughly crushed
2 teaspoons cumin seeds, roughly crushed

Preheat the oven to 180°C. Cut all the skin from the pumpkin. In a bowl, toss the slices in a few splashes of oil with the crushed coriander and cumin seeds, then lay them on roasting trays. Roast for about an hour, or until the pumpkin is gently browned. Eat with roast lamb.

ROASTED PUMPKIN SALAD

If you've still got a kilo of roast pumpkin left over, try this as an instant lunch: simply mix together a bowl of roast pumpkin slices with a torn-up ball of mozzarella, some lovely ripe tomatoes, a handful of basil, a couple of spoonfuls of Greek yoghurt and a few slugs of extra virgin olive oil.

ROASTED PUMPKIN AND LEMON TAGLIATELLE

1kg pumpkin, cut into thick slices
6 garlic cloves, unpeeled
a small handful of sage leaves, finely chopped
zest and juice of 2 lemons
olive oil
salt and freshly ground black pepper
tagliatelle, prepared according to your liking
Parmesan, grated, to serve

Preheat the oven to 180°C. Cut all the skin from the pumpkin, toss the slices and unpeeled garlic cloves in a few splashes of oil and lay them on roasting trays. Cover with foil and roast for about an hour or until the pumpkin is nicely browned.

Squeeze the garlic from the cloves and put in a bowl with the roasted pumpkin, chopped sage, lemon zest and juice, a generous splash of olive oil, and seasoning and mash together. Mix into the cooked pasta, add grated Parmesan and serve.

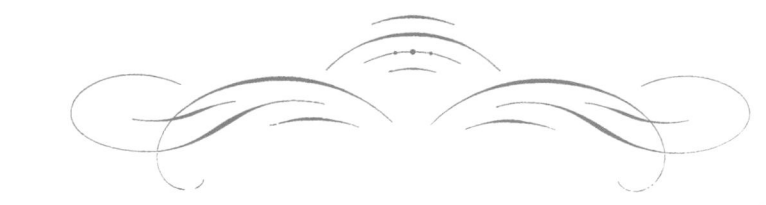

PAPPA AL POMODORO
(LIQUID PIZZA)

This is a whopping great gutsy soup for a cold day when you feel in need of either some zip, or a big cuddle. Essentially, it's a tomato soup thickened with hunks of bread, and it's especially delicious made with sourdough – stale or not. The bread soaks up all the flavours and somehow melts into a sublime silkiness. I can't help thinking that it's essentially a liquid pizza. In a good way.

This is made with both tinned tomatoes and some extra fresh tomatoes that you roast beforehand to give a really deep flavour.

SERVES 4

500g ripe tomatoes, quartered*
100ml (plus 2 tablespoons)
 extra virgin olive oil
1 teaspoon sugar
salt and freshly ground black pepper
4 garlic cloves, peeled and finely sliced
a handful of sage leaves,
 roughly chopped
1 teaspoon chopped red chilli (optional)
250g bread – preferably sourdough
or ciabatta – torn into shreds
2 x 400g tins of tomatoes
salt and pepper
fresh bread and butter, to serve

* If you're pushed for time or you're making this in winter when really good ripe tomatoes are hard to find, you can cheat by using an extra tin of tomatoes and skipping the roasting.

Preheat the oven to 190°C. In a roasting tray, toss the fresh tomatoes in a splash of olive oil, the sugar, salt and pepper and roast them uncovered for 20 minutes.

While the tomatoes are roasting, heat a large, thick-based saucepan and add 50ml of the olive oil, the garlic, sage leaves (reserving some to use as a garnish) and chilli (if using). Cook over a low heat to soften them for a few minutes, but don't let them brown, then add the bread and toss it in the oil. Add the tinned tomatoes and break them up with a wooden spoon. Fill a tin with water and add that too. Simmer for about 15 minutes.

Remove the tomatoes from the oven and stir them into the soup, along with any juices from the roasting tray. (Peel the tomatoes if you prefer them that way – I like the texture of them unpeeled.) Pour over a further 50ml olive oil and check the seasoning (it usually needs salt) and consistency, adding some more water if necessary – it should have the texture of thin porridge. Stir again and simmer for a further 2 minutes.

Pour the soup into warmed bowls and drizzle a teaspoon of olive oil and scatter extra sage leaves over each bowl. Serve with extra bread and butter.

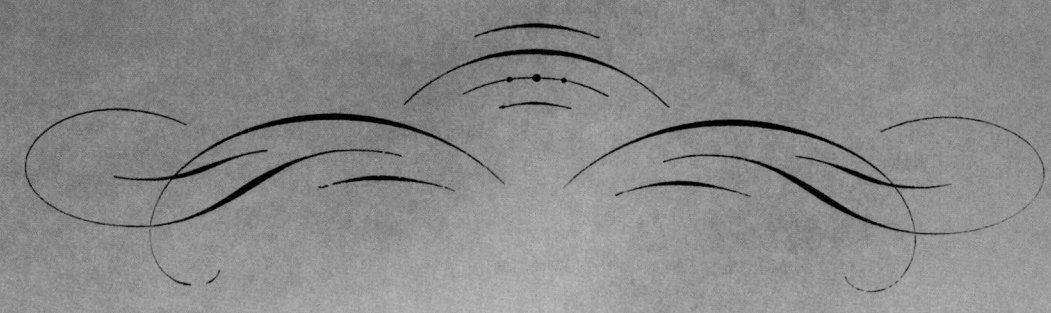

4

STARTERS

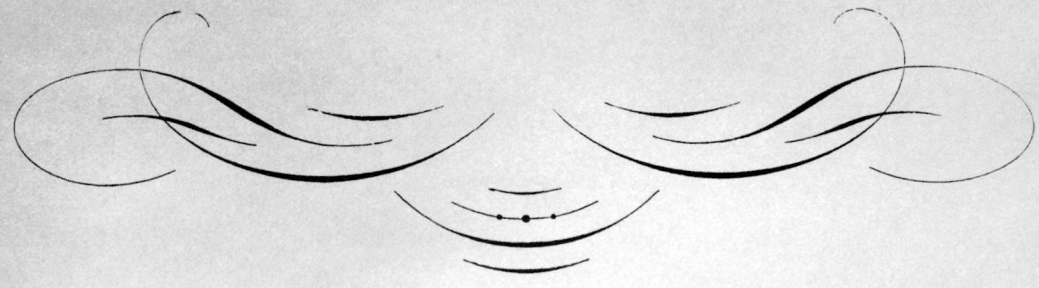

OKAY, HOLD ONTO YOUR SEATS, because it's time to spread our wings and play with some of the world's most wonderful, most extraordinary ingredients. Herein lie razor clams, frogs' legs, jellyfish and stuffed courgette flowers. Obviously some of them are more exotic and locally available than others, but it doesn't take much asking around or internet searching to lay your hands on anything here. If unfamiliar foods put the willies up you, don't worry, because there are also some simple, cheap and familiar foods in this chapter. Any butcher worth his chops will get some veal bones for your bone marrow and even whole artichokes are a hands-on culinary extravaganza as long as you serve them as described here: whole and unadorned rather than fiddled with as a restaurant chef must, for fear of making a mess of the maître d's napiery.

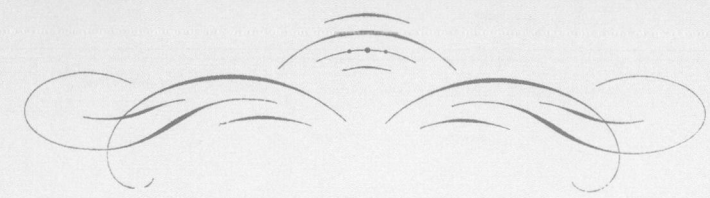

WHOLE ARTICHOKES WITH LEMON BUTTER

Eating whole artichokes is great, messy, interactive fun, but is it really that extraordinary? Well, that depends on your frame of reference. You're probably a hip, adventurous, sophisticated eater already, but I've found that even though loads of my friends have had prepared artichoke hearts in the past, the majority of them have never faced the whole shebang, leaves and all, before, and they're always excited when trying it for the first time. And, in case you haven't been introduced to these strange and wonderful vegetables, I'd be honoured to take that responsibility.

PER PERSON:

1 large globe artichoke
50g butter
salt and freshly ground black pepper
zest and juice of ½ lemon

Pull any straggly leaves off the artichokes then chop the thick stalk off. Bring a large pan of salted water to the boil then add the artichokes. Bring back to the boil and cook for 20–25 minutes, checking after 20 minutes by pulling off one of the larger leaves in the middle. The base of the leaf (where it attaches to the core) should be soft enough to easily bite a little nugget of artichoke flesh from one side with your teeth. When they are ready, remove and place upside-down to drain for 5 minutes, then place them upright on plates.

In a small saucepan, melt the butter with a large pinch of salt and pepper, add the lemon juice and zest and pour over the middle of the artichoke so that it soaks in. Serve with a large bowl in the centre of the table for the discarded leaves.

HOW TO TACKLE A WHOLE ARTICHOKE

Pull off the outer leaves one at a time, dipping each one in the butter and biting the little lump of tender flesh from the inside edge with your teeth before discarding. Keep going until you get to the tiny little leaves with no flesh on in the middle (they are often purple and aren't really edible).

Using a knife, cut a bowl shape out of the middle of the artichoke, taking out the centre leaves and the spikes that are underneath them. Throw this away and scrape any stubby bits of choke from the middle too. You will be left with a bowl-shaped section. This is the heart – the delicious central part that's so revered. Chop or tear it into chunks, dip in the remaining butter and eat.

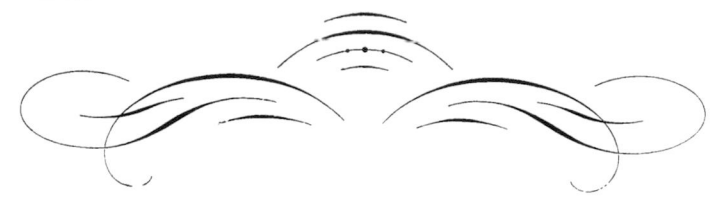

FLOWER SALADS

You've probably heard of edible nasturtiums but there's a surprising variety of other flowers that are good to eat, too. You can add them to salads, or make entire flower dishes, like the one below. I love borage, elderflowers and dandelions, in particular, and I'll nick the roses when Georgia isn't looking, but I've always thought it a terrible shame that buttercups are poisonous. You should remove greenery and the pistils and stamen from most flowers before you eat them.

You should be sensible when choosing flowers to eat – for example, picking wild flowers is illegal in the UK (although I'm sure no-one would begrudge you a few dandelions) and you should only use flowers that you know haven't been sprayed with a non-food-grade pesticide. For these reasons, it's probably best to avoid kerbside flowers. In case you fancy experimenting with other flowers, here's a brief and incomplete guide to some interesting flowers that are edible and some that aren't:

EDIBLE
● borage (great for G&T or in Pimm's ● chives
● dandelions ● elderflowers ● primrose and evening
primrose ● scented geraniums (petals only) ● hollyhocks
● lavender ● rosemary ● roses (petals only – remove
the light-coloured 'heel' from the base of each petal)
● marigolds (petals only) ● nasturtiums
● chrysanthemums (petals only)

NOT EDIBLE
● anemone ● lily of the valley ● foxglove
● ivy ● hyacinth ● iris ● daffodils ● buttercup
● mistletoe ● wisteria

DANDELION AND ELDERFLOWER SALAD

You can eat the entire flowers of elderflowers and both the flowers and leaves of dandelions and so this is a particularly good combination. Dandelions have a sort of bittersweet taste and elderflowers, which flower in late spring to early summer, are just sublimely sweet and floral-tasting.

250g dandelion leaves, washed
   (use rocket salad if you can't find these)
2 large handfuls whole dandelion
   flowers, cut off as close to the flower
   as possible, all stems and green parts
   from around the neck removed
2 large handfuls of elderflowers,
   checked for bugs, and picked off the stalks

FOR THE DRESSING
1 tablespoon orange juice
1 teaspoon walnut oil
1 teaspoon white wine vinegar
salt and freshly ground black pepper

Put the dandelion flowers and leaves in a bowl. Combine the dressing ingredients together in a small bowl and mix thoroughly. Pour over the salad and toss together, then scatter the elderflowers on top.

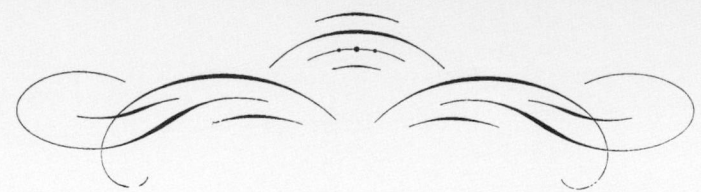

CLAMS WITH LINGUINE (LINGUINE ALLE VONGOLE)

You can make this recipe with pretty much any type of clams: posh and expensive palourdes, sweet little triangular tellines, or cheap and unassuming cockles. Cockles never get the respect they deserve in the UK despite the fact that vast amounts are gathered from British sands, tickled out from where they hide, happily filtering plankton from the seawater. They are fabulous, as well as being very cheap in this country– more than three-quarters of all British cockles are exported to countries such as Spain and France where they are revered. Tellines are wonderful little fellas – they're about the size of a thumbnail and taste extraordinarily sweet in your mouth – but can be hard to track down, so cockles are really where it's at.

The experience of eating clams in spaghetti is a wonderful journey in its own right, as you ferret around for the little shells before gnawing out their precious meat and getting your fingers deliciously flavoured for licking. The one thing you need to be really careful about is washing them: cockles can carry a fair amount of sand, and there's nothing quite as annoying as a gritty lunch.

SERVES 6

500g dried linguine or spaghetti
75ml extra-virgin olive oil
6 fat garlic cloves, thinly sliced
½ red chilli, deseeded and finely sliced
a large handful of parsley leaves, finely chopped
1.2kg cockles, or other clams,
    thoroughly washed
2 tablespoons white wine
salt and freshly ground black pepper

Boil the pasta until just *al dente* (no more, as it will need to stand for a few minutes while you do the next bit), then drain and return to the pan, toss in a few splashes of olive oil and cover the pan to keep it warm.

Put a large saucepan over a medium heat, add the olive oil, garlic and chilli and gently fry for 2–3 minutes until the garlic starts to soften but not brown. Add the parsley, cockles, wine, salt and pepper and stir it all through.

Cover the pan and continue to cook for 5–6 minutes, giving the pan a gentle shake every now and then until all the cockles have opened.

Add the drained pasta, stir through, check the seasoning and serve. You'll need a bowl in which to throw the empty shells, and some napkins for wiping sticky fingers.

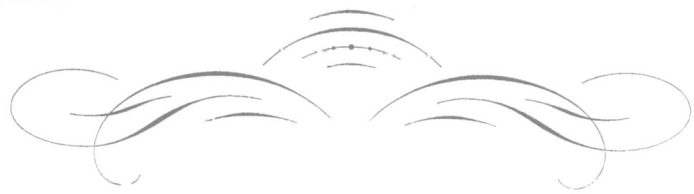

APPLE CAVIAR

I'll be straight with you here: for most of this book I have gone to huge lengths to make sure that all the flights of fancy and extraordinary recipes and techniques are easy, practical and achievable, using ingredients that you can find in your local supermarket or corner shop. This recipe is different.

This is a brilliant, fun recipe, and its fascination lies in the scientific intricacy of an intriguing arm of molecular gastronomy known as spherification. You can buy all the strange-sounding ingredients online from a company called MSK (see Suppliers, page 218), which provides great chefs with weird and wonderful specialist bits and bobs. You specifically need sodium alginate (which helps turn liquids into thick gels) and calcium chloride (which hardens the outer shell of the gel on contact, creating the caviar effect). You'll also need a syringe to use as a very controllable dropper (easily available from your local chemist for measuring children's medicines) and some digital scales that read small amounts down to 1g.

SOME USEFUL TIPS
- Read the recipe carefully and buy or gather all your ingredients before trying the recipe.
- This recipe might not work with very hard tap water (although I've never had any problems with London tap water!) If you think your water is very hard, you might be better off using bottled mineral water or distilled water.
- The calcium chloride works best if your base juice is a little acidic like apple, orange or blackcurrant, so if you are tempted to try other flavours, check them out first. Also, very high sugar solutions sometimes won't work.
- Don't be tempted to reduce the juice to a syrup in an attempt to make the flavour stronger as this may unbalance the reaction and your caviar might not set. You need a high free water content (i.e. not too sugary) in your base syrup to begin with.
- Once you've got the hang of it, you can do the final part at the table, should you fancy a bit of theatre.

300ml apple juice
3g sodium alginate
20g caster sugar
5 drops green food colouring

FOR THE CALCIUM BATH
500ml water
5g calcium chloride
10 drops green food colouring

FOR STORAGE
250ml apple juice
a few drops of green colouring

Pour the apple juice into a bowl. Mix the sodium alginate and sugar together in another bowl, then slowly add it to the juice a little at a time while whisking it (do this in an electric food mixer if you have one) trying to avoid it making lumps. Add the food colouring and whisk gently for 5 minutes on the slowest setting, then leave the mixture to stand for 10 minutes as it thickens to a lump-free gel.

Make up the calcium bath in a bowl by mixing the calcium chloride and food colouring into the water and stirring until dissolved. Pour the 250ml apple juice (for storage) into a bowl and set aside.

Draw the syrup into a syringe and, holding the tip of the syringe 10cm above the bowl, squeeze it slowly to drop regular, steady drops into the calcium bath. Gently stir the water as you do this to help the drops turn into spheres.

The little balls of 'caviar' shouldn't stay in the calcium bath for more than 3 minutes or they will solidify too much. After each syringe-full, scoop them up using a sieve or tea-strainer, rinse in a little cold water, then store in the bowl of fruit juice, adding a few drops of the food colouring to match the colour of the caviar (otherwise the colour will slowly fade). The caviar will keep for 2–3 days in the fridge.

Serve the caviar as a topping for pâté or soft cheeses, or to give an extraordinary twist to a sushi or sashimi party. It makes an extraordinary garnish for pork chops, too.

VARIATION: BLACKCURRANT CAVIAR
Replace the apple juice with blackcurrant juice, made up to double the normal concentration, and use purple food colouring instead of green. Great with turkey.

VARIATION: ORANGE CAVIAR
Replace the apple juice with orange juice (the sort with no bits), use orange food colouring instead of green and add 2 drops of orange oil (optional). Great with roast duck.

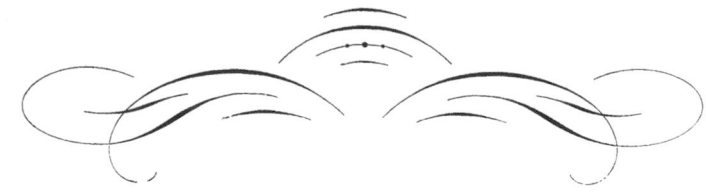

CRISPY JELLYFISH AND BEANSPROUT SALAD

Jellyfish are one of the world's great untapped food resources (another is insects, see page 34), and they are in abundance in the oceans, so eating them doesn't harm biodiversity. And if you've ever been stung by one, here's your chance for a bit of *schadenfreude*.

Edible jellyfish are neither jellylike, nor do they sting. In fact they are relatively fat-free and taste-free, so you eat them for their high protein content and their extraordinary texture, which is both rubbery and crunchy at the same time. You can buy them from many Chinese and Thai supermarkets and they come in two versions: 'Jellyfish Salad', which is ready to eat, and 'Salted', which has been preserved in salt and needs to be soaked for 3–4 hours before use.

I'm determined to find more uses for jellyfish, but I've been unable to crack new recipes. I tried jellyfish lollipops, but they didn't catch on, and I even spent several days trying to perfect a recipe for jellyfish burgers. I did finally manage it (the recipe's on my web site at www.thegastronaut.com) but they were annoyingly complicated. If you come up with any new uses, I'd love to know about them. In the meantime, stick to this salad – it's great!

SOME JELLYFISH FACTS

1. Jellyfish have no brain and no central nervous system, with the exception of the box jellyfish, which has four independent brains. (I'm in awe: imagine ordering dinner at a restaurant when you've got four brains!)
2. They are ninety-five per cent water and five per cent protein.
3. The *Turritopsis nutricula* jellyfish seems to be the only immortal being on the planet: it has the ability to rejuvenate itself when it becomes an adult. Weird, huh?

SERVES 4

FOR THE SALAD

150g pack ('ready to eat') jellyfish salad
150g beansprouts
1 carrot, peeled and finely shredded
1 celery stalk, washed and finely sliced
a small handful of coriander leaves,
    roughly chopped
2 spring onions, finely sliced

FOR THE DRESSING

1 tablespoon vegetable oil
1 teaspoon Thai fish sauce (nam pla)
1 teaspoon toasted sesame oil
1 teaspoon lime juice
½ teaspoon red chilli, finely chopped

Put the jellyfish in a colander and rinse with cold water, then set aside to drain. Combine all the salad ingredients in a large bowl.

Put all the dressing ingredients in a lidded jar and shake well to mix them together. Make sure the jellyfish is dry, then add to the salad, pour over the dressing and toss everything together.

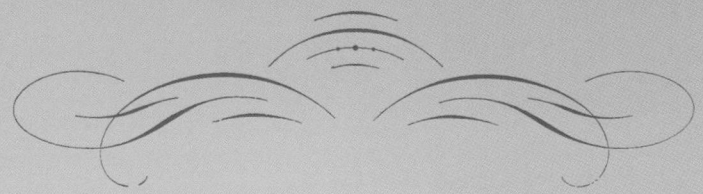

SALMON CAVIAR TAGLIATELLE

This spectacular dish is delicate and full-flavoured, yet needs little planning and is simple to cook. Salmon eggs in jars last for about a year in the fridge, so it's worth keeping some to hand for when inspiration strikes. You can also make this with lumpfish caviar, which is cheap and also delicious, though it lacks the luxuriousness of salmon. Avoid adding extra salt (without tasting first) as the salmon and the eggs are both salty.

SERVES 4 AS A STARTER OR 2 AS A RICH MAIN COURSE

250g tagliatelle or fettucine
50g butter
a handful of parsley, finely chopped
150g crème fraîche
1 tablespoon lemon juice (one good
squeeze should do it)
50g jar salmon caviar (or lumpfish caviar)
100g smoked salmon, cut into thin ribbons
freshly ground black pepper

Cook the pasta in a large pan of boiling water until it's *al dente*. Drain (reserving a cupful of the cooking water), return to the pan, add half of the butter and toss to combine. Cover the pan to keep the pasta warm.

In a large frying pan, melt the remainder of the butter over a low heat, then add the parsley, crème fraîche and lemon juice and stir through. Turn the heat off, then add the pasta and smoked salmon and toss it through the creamy mixture until thoroughly coated. Add a few splashes of the pasta cooking water *only* if it seems too dry, then add half the salmon caviar and mix very gently.

Serve on warm plates, topped with the remaining caviar (otherwise it all falls to the bottom) and some freshly ground black pepper.

RAZOR CLAMS

Razor clams are beautiful and extraordinary, and occasionally they can look just a little bit rude. They are also becoming more common in fishmongers and restaurants, and not before time, because they are sweet and delicious when cooked right – i.e. quickly and simply. The best I've ever tasted were at The Drapers Arms pub in Islington, London, and this is pretty much how they were cooked, with just butter, olive oil, lemon and garlic.

SERVES 6

100g butter
a splash of olive oil
6 garlic cloves, finely chopped
24 razor clams, thoroughly washed
   in lots of water to remove sand
a handful of fresh parsley, finely chopped
lemon wedges, bread and butter, to serve

Heat a wide, thick-based pan over a medium heat and add the butter, olive oil and garlic. Fry the garlic gently for 2–3 minutes, then turn the heat up and add the clams, turning them very gently in the butter so that they don't break. Fry them for 2–4 minutes or until they all open. Don't cook for any longer than is absolutely necessary as they will turn rubbery. Serve on warm plates, spoon over the pan juices and scatter over the chopped parsley. Serve with the lemon wedges, bread and butter.

FROGS' LEGS

One of the great rules about food is that the golden combination of butter, garlic, parsley and salt will scatter culinary stardust on pretty much any fish or meat, and quite a few vegetables too, come to think of it. I don't think that's the only reason that frogs' legs are so delicious, but it certainly doesn't hurt. They make good eating and taste like very dainty chicken. And of course I'd be obtuse if I didn't acknowledge that there's a frisson of *something* when you eat a frog.

You can buy frozen frogs' legs from many fishmongers (despite the fact that they aren't fish) and they are easily available online, too (see Suppliers, page 218). If you find yourself in France, it goes without saying that you'll find them in the freezer sections of most big supermarkets, marked as 'grenouilles'.

SERVES 6

2 tablespoons olive oil
18 frogs' legs, defrosted from frozen and
    thoroughly dried
4 fat garlic cloves, peeled and finely chopped
100g plain flour
salt and freshly ground black pepper
150g butter
a handful of fresh parsley leaves, finely chopped
rocket salad and slices of lemon, to serve

Put the olive oil in a large bowl, add the frogs' legs and toss until thinly coated. In another bowl, mix the chopped garlic with the flour and plenty of salt and pepper. Toss the frogs' legs around in the flour until thoroughly coated.

Melt the butter in a large saucepan and fry the frogs' legs, six at a time (otherwise they'll cook too slowly and end up chewy), over a medium heat until they are nicely browned and crispy on the outside.

Drain each batch on kitchen paper to remove excess oil, then season again with salt and pepper to taste and scatter with parsley. Serve with a rocket salad and slices of lemon.

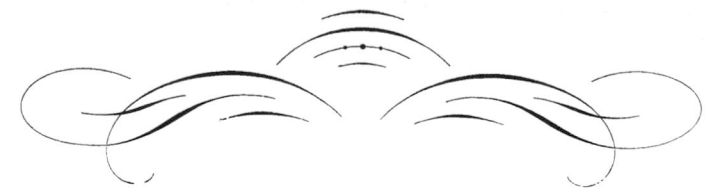

SWEETLY SPICED CHICKEN LOLLIPOPS

This is an unashamedly kid-friendly version of chicken drumsticks that my little girls adore, not just because the word 'lollipop', makes them absurdly excited (the girls, not the drumsticks), but also because they are sweetly, stickily delicious. And, in fact, there's a good culinary reason for this method: when you take the skin off chicken, you allow better access for the marinades to flavour the meat. The lollipoppiness of these comes from the way you turn the skinned drumstick half inside out, leaving a handle to hold as you eat the marinated ball of chicken at the other end.

I've given a recipe for a delicious fragrant teriyaki-style marinade, but you could use a ready-made bottled marinade, or even just a bottle of sweet chilli sauce to pretty good effect. I particularly love a hot smoked paprika and garlic version (just mix them with lots of olive oil and lemon juice), but its pretty pokey for young palates, so we'll stick to the milder one here.

MAKES 8 DRUMSTICKS

8 chicken drumsticks, skinned

FOR THE MARINADE
2 garlic cloves, crushed
5cm thumb of ginger, peeled and grated
2 lemongrass stalks, outer leaves removed
    and very finely chopped (optional)
zest and juice of 1 lime
4 tablespoons runny honey
4 tablespoons soy sauce
4 tablespoons vegetable oil

Preheat the oven to 200°C. Preparing the drumsticks is a little fiddly the first time you try it, but just imagine you're turning them inside-out like a sock. Take a skinned drumstick and, using a small knife, cut and scrape away the meat from around the bone only at the thick meaty end, then push the meat up towards the thinner end and over the knuckle. It should remain still attached to the knuckle. Don't worry about making them look smart.

To make the marinade, combine all the ingredients in a bowl and mix together with a fork. Place your drumsticks in a bowl small enough for them to fit snugly, meat end down, then pour over the marinade. Cover and refrigerate for at least 20 minutes, and preferably 2 hours or longer.

Rip some foil to wrap around the bones so they don't burn, then turn the drumsticks in the marinade one last time and place them in a roasting tray. Roast for about 40 minutes (depending on the size of your drumsticks), checking them twice to ensure they haven't dried out, and basting as needed.

While the drumsticks are roasting, pour the remaining marinade into a small saucepan and simmer for 2 minutes to make a dipping sauce, adding a splash of water if it seems too dry.

Check the drumsticks are cooked through, then remove from the oven, remove the foil and leave to cool for about 10 minutes until they can be held comfortably without burning little hands. Serve with the dipping sauce.

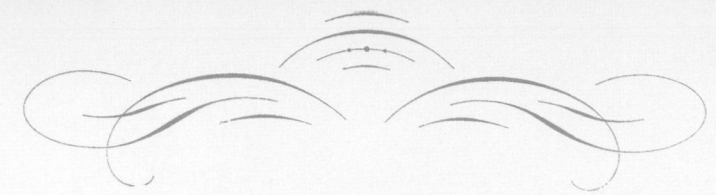

LAMB'S TESTICLES

I get quite evangelical about trying new food. After all, someone had to make some huge leaps in experimenting with cocoa to end up with chocolate. (Have you ever tasted raw cocoa or cocoa nibs? They're horrible!) And even the potato started off as an odd, wizened little tuber that was originally though to be inherently evil. We have a responsibility to the world to come up with some sort of solution to our food problems, so we must continue to experiment and explore.

I'm not sure if testicle-eating will solve the world's food problems, but it will probably help. They are delicate (similar to sweetbreads, although the myth that sweetbreads *are* testicles is untrue – see the recipe on page 159) and delicious and it would be a tragedy if protein of this quality were thrown away. In the past, I've followed complicated recipes for soaking and blanching them for hours, but after necking more than my fair share of nuts over the past few years I've realised that none of that's really necessary. I just peel them of the outer membrane (come on, now, be bold) and then cook them in the holy culinary trinity; butter, garlic and parsley.

You can ask your local butcher for lamb's testicles, or look for them in shops in ethnic areas where lamb is very popular. I'm very lucky to live in an area of London that has lots of Turkish shops, and the butchers often stock lamb's testicles very cheaply (you have to ask for lamb 'eggs', oddly enough).

SERVES 6

4 lamb's testicles
50g plain flour
4 garlic cloves, peeled and finely sliced
1 teaspoon salt
freshly ground black pepper
50g butter
2 tablespoons olive oil
crisp salad with some green beans added, to serve

Using a sharp knife, cut the testicles in half lengthways, then pull the thick membranes off, together with any veiny bits at the end. The first one will be fiddly, but you'll soon get the hang of it. You'll reveal a soft and light-pink interior. Discard the membranes and cut the soft interiors into chunks the size of your thumb.

In a large bowl, mix the flour, garlic, salt and a good few grinds of black pepper. Add the testicles and toss them around in the flour until well coated. (They may start to seem sticky, but that's fine.)

Heat the butter and oil together in a large frying pan over a medium heat, then fry the testicles a handful at a time. (Don't cram them into the frying pan or they won't fry properly.) When they are lightly browned, remove and place on kitchen paper to drain any excess fat. Cook the remainder, adding more oil if needed. Check the seasoning and add more salt and pepper if desired. Serve with a crisp bean salad.

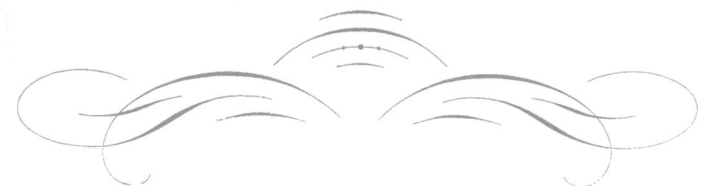

PIGS' TROTTERS

If you find jellied pigs' trotters for sale, don't turn your nose up but instead consider yourself very lucky. Snap them up, run home and call some adventurous friends over for supper, because you've found a unique and special food. I'll admit that when I first ate trotters I was confused that there was no meat on them. It takes a trusted friend (that'll be me, now that I've eaten more than my fair share of these beauties) to explain that what you're eating is the slow-cooked, tender skin and the gelatinous parts of the trotter, which are all unctuous goodness and deep flavour. It's a love-it-or-hate-it kind of experience, but anyone who enjoys offal – or who hates it when people throw away good food just because it's unfamiliar – should revel in eating them.

It's very easy to find cooked pigs' trotters in France, Spain and Italy, although unfortunately less so in the UK at the moment. They take a long time to cook from scratch (several hours of slow boiling), but luckily they also come pre-cooked, set in their own gelatine created by the cooking process. If they haven't already been halved lengthways, ask the butcher to do this for you, then just heat them up with some toppings before eating with lots of crusty bread.

SERVES 6

3 cooked pigs' trotters, halved lengthways
2 garlic cloves, crushed
a handful of parsley leaves, finely chopped
75g butter
2 handfuls of breadcrumbs
salt and freshly ground black pepper
gherkins, mustard and lots of crusty
   French bread and butter, to serve

Remove the pigs' trotters from the fridge 20 minutes before cooking. Preheat the oven to 200°C. Lay the trotters cut-side up in a roasting tin and chuck the garlic and half the parsley over them. Cut thin slivers of butter and lay them on top, then sprinkle with breadcrumbs, salt and pepper. Roast uncovered for 20 minutes, then scatter with the remaining parsley and serve with bread and butter.

5

INTERACTIVE MEALS

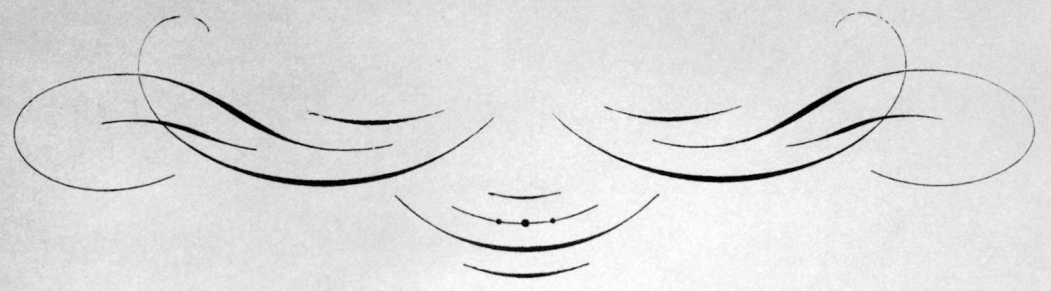

WELCOME TO MY WORLD. I love these interactive meals because my family and friends know that whenever I serve them, supper is bound to turn into a party, and when my family and friends are *that* happy (and *that* noisy) I get a rush of exhilaration and I know that everything is right with the world. The word 'interactive' may sound a little odd, seeing as we all interact with our food by putting it into our mouths, but this chapter is really about the communal act of cooking, where everyone lends a hand. Most of these dishes go one cheeky step further by getting everyone to grips with the raw ingredients themselves, in order to cook their own meal. Oh, and if any single recipe defines this book, it's probably Shabu-shabu, with its hands-on DIY tabletop free-for-all mayhem. None of the ingredients in it are particularly unusual; it's all in the delivery. If you only make one meal from this book, make Shabu-shabu. You and your friends will neither regret it nor forget it.

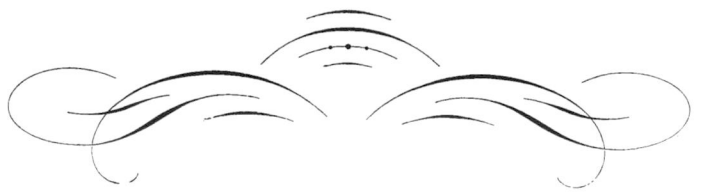

SAVOURY DIY TARTS

This is the perfect solution for the times when you've invited a friend for dinner who happens to be a brilliant cook, or – heaven forbid – a celebrity chef. Instead of jumping through hoops trying to think of something ridiculously extravagant to match their expectations, get them to do the work!

What you do is place all the ingredients on the table, including a chunk of puff pastry, then hand around one greased baking sheet between each pair of people and let them make their own tarts. They do all the hard work, indulging their gustatory preferences and creating a little work of wonder, and all you have to do is slip it in the oven for about 15 minutes then deliver it back to them. DIY Pizza is a variation on this theme, but DIY Tarts are even easier, because it's pretty much impossible to mess up a puff pastry tarlet (unlike a pizza).

(You can, of course, do dessert in the same way: see Sweet DIY Tarts, page 192.)

SERVES 6

500g pack of puff pastry
flour, for dusting
butter, for greasing
olive oil
salt and freshly ground black pepper
rocket salad, to serve

FOR THE TOPPINGS (AS WITH PIZZAS, YOU WON'T NEED MUCH OF EACH)
goat's cheese, cut or ripped into chunks
fresh rosemary, thyme and basil
red peppers, sliced
asparagus, blanched
mushrooms, sliced and tossed in a little
   olive oil
peas, broad beans or spinach
very sweet tomatoes
slices of salami, chorizo or cured ham
sweet chillies

Preheat the oven to 200°C. On a floured surface, roll the pastry out to the thickness of about 3mm and then cut into 6 large slices or 12 small ones in whichever shapes you fancy. Lightly grease two or three baking sheets, dust with a little plain flour, and place the pastry pieces on them with a good 2cm gap between each. Place the baking sheets on the table along with the topping ingredients.

Encourage your friends to experiment with the toppings, advising them that delicate ingredients like ham, basil or spinach should be at the bottom or they will dry out. Season the finished tarts, then take the baking sheets away and bake uncovered for 15–18 minutes until crusty and golden around the edges.

Drizzle a little olive oil over the tarts and return them to your friends piping hot. Serve with some rocket salad.

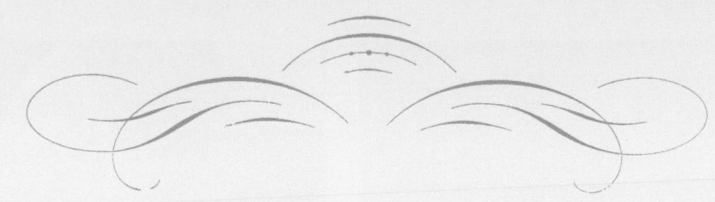

SALMON TARTARE WITH CUCUMBER AND GREEN BEAN SALAD

One of the great things about steak tartare is the DIY aspect – being given all the flavouring ingredients so you can essentially build it yourself – and the same is true with salmon tartare.

This is much less daunting to make at home than steak tartare: it ranges from exquisitely delicate to punchy and herby, depending on how you throw yours together. The fun lies in putting all the ingredients on the table ready for your friends to dig into as they wish.

HINT: if you have a circular table you can just put everything in the middle, with a plate in front of each of your friends, and let them get on with it. However, if your table is rectangular (like mine), you really need to split the ingredients into several bowls so they are easy for everyone to reach.

SERVES 6

800g very fresh salmon fillet, skinned and boned
1 teaspoon caster sugar
½ teaspoon salt

FOR THE SALAD
400g green beans
1 whole cucumber, peeled
a handful of fresh dill, chopped
2 tablespoons olive oil
2 teaspoons white wine vinegar (or sherry vinegar)
salt and freshly ground black pepper

TO SERVE
sourdough toast and butter
1 tablespoon finely chopped shallots
a large handful of parsley leaves, finely chopped
2 lemons, each cut into 6 segments
2 tablespoons capers, finely chopped
2 tablespoons gherkins, finely chopped
Tabasco
Worcester sauce

Using a sharp knife, chop the salmon into small pieces about the size of coffee beans (don't use a food processor as this will create a paste – you want to keep the texture of the fish). Put the salmon pieces in a bowl, sprinkle over the sugar and salt and stir thoroughly to combine. Cover and refrigerate for about 30 minutes (which is just about the right amount of time to do all of the following).

To make the salad, boil or steam the green beans until just tender then rinse in plenty of cold water (they need to be cool, but this also keeps them vividly green). Shave the whole cucumber into very thin slivers using a vegetable peeler or mandolin. Put the beans and cucumber into a large bowl. Combine the dill, olive oil, vinegar, a pinch of salt and a few grinds of black pepper in a bowl and mix thoroughly. Pour this over the cucumbers and beans and toss through.

Grill slices of sourdough bread on a ridged grill pan or in a toaster. Put the shallots, parsley, lemon segments, capers and gherkins into separate small bowls.

Give each person a plate or bowl and a spoon for serving. Put the salmon, salads and toasts on the table in large bowls and place all the other ingredients on the table around them. Everyone builds their personal bowl of tartare to their liking (just as with beef tartare), starting with a small mound of salmon. The flavourings should be mixed into the salmon to each individual's liking, just as with beef tartare. Start with a squeeze of lemon and add the other flavourings as you see fit.

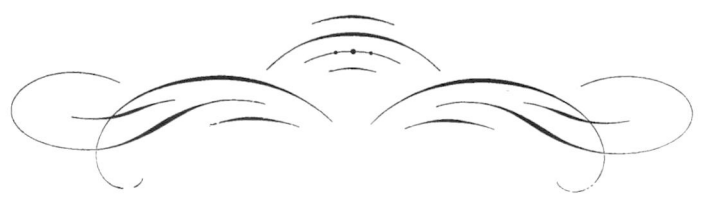

VEGETABLE INSTRUMENTS

Yup, with a little whittling you can make a carrot into a flute, a pumpkin into a bongo and a butternut squash into an unholy sounding, crazy-assed bassoon! It may sound like a ridiculous use for fresh veg, but it does have a long and noble history – the Indian snake-charmer's *pungi* is made from the bottle gourd, the Japanese *tonkori* has strings of vegetable fibres (although it does make a *horrible* sound) and the Votic bagpipe *rakkopilli* was made of a pig's bladder. People have been making sweet harmony from their lunch for thousands of years, and there's even a modern orchestra that plays exclusively on vegetables – the Viennese Vegetable Orchestra – and very good they are too.

There are lots of different ways you can tease simple tunes out of fruit and veg, but the sweeter and more controllable the sound, the more complex the design. I'm going to talk you through some basic instruments to get you started. The flow of air in these things can be complex and variable, so you have to be prepared to ditch the occasional one for the pot without getting so much as a squeak out of it. Plan to make several for sharing anyway. Sometimes it's just whittler's luck.

A note on storage: to stop your completed instruments going brown and floppy, keep them in a bowl of water in the fridge.

When you've finished using your vegetables for making beautiful music, don't throw them away; they can still make a wonderful soup as long as you boil them thoroughly to sterilise them!

BUTTERNUT SQUASH PUNGI/BASSOON

This one is dead easy. You need a long butternut squash (for some reason the longer ones seem to give you a better range of notes) or a huge mooli. You'll also need some straws to use for mouthpieces (they work like the double reed on an oboe or bassoon), an electric drill, a medium-sized drill bit the same width as your straws (usually a number 4) and an extra-long wide drill bit for hollowing out.

If you are using a squash, cut off 5cm from the thick end at the bottom – you need to cut off enough to expose the chamber holding the seeds. Then scoop out the seeds.

Drill a small hole from the top (the thin end) towards the thicker end, going as far as you can with the drill bit. Then turn the squash over, change to the large drill bit and drill a larger chamber from the thicker end of the squash or mooli up to meet the thinner hole. Check that the hole goes all the way through and that it's clear of vegetable debris.

Cut the straw in half and then chop one end into a sharp arrow shape. Push the other end into the squash or mooli and blow. Again, it takes a little experimentation to find the pitch, playing with the depth of the straw and the force of blow, but you should be able to replicate the sound of a snake-charmer's pungi.

PUMPKIN OR CELERIAC BONGOS

This is even easier. You need two or three good, very solid fruit for this, and they should be of different sizes to give you different notes. Cut a 6cm-diameter hole from the base end and then use a teaspoon and small sharp knife to remove the stringy innards without destroying the structural integrity of the vegetable – it should be sturdy, but hollow. Experiment with playing it, covering the opening a little with one hand as you pat the bongo with carrots, hands or wooden spoons.

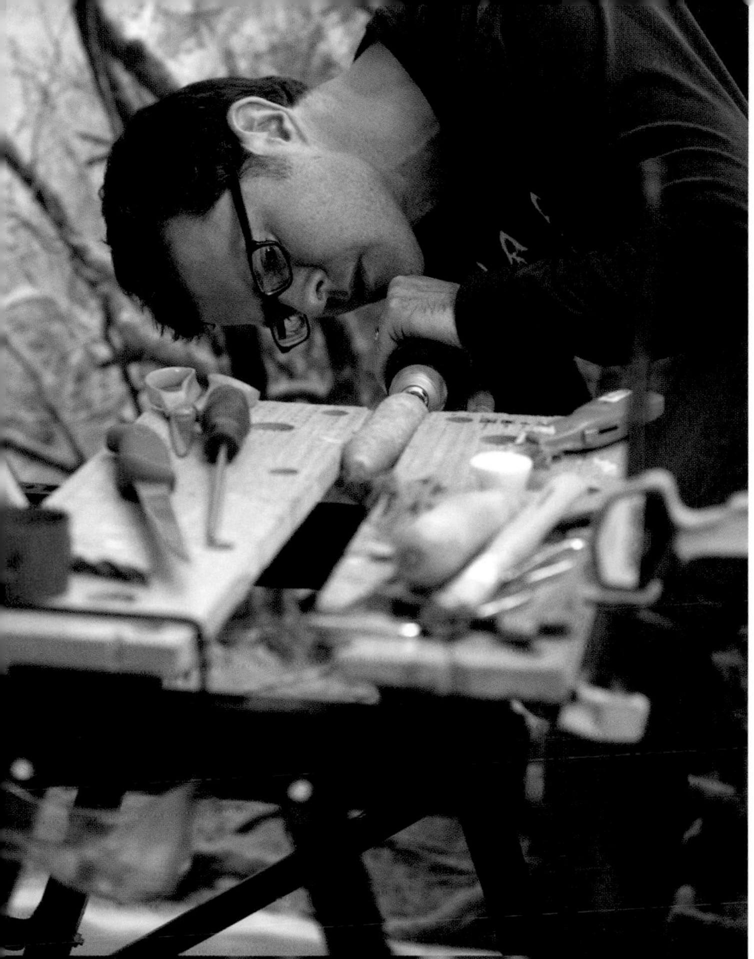

CARROT FLUTES

This is an end-blown flute – a sort of cross between a flute and a whistle. You hold it with the carrot pointing directly away from you, but the sound comes by blowing *over* a hole rather than into it.

You'll need some large carrots, a small sharp knife and a drill with various drill bits, including a very long one.

Firstly, cut a short slice off each end to flatten it ready for drilling. Then drill a wide (12mm) hole all the way through your carrot. The easiest way is to start with a small drill bit and then change it for a long, thick one. If your drill bit is shorter than the carrot you'll have to do one end first, then continue from the other end. Be careful, please, and operate the drill only at low speed.

Now drill three finger holes somewhere near the middle of the carrot using a medium (6mm) drill bit. To tell the truth, the finger holes are a bit hit-and-miss, and their effectiveness depends on the aerodynamics within your particular carrot. You'll probably find that covering some of the air holes changes the pitch but covering others makes no difference.

 Now create the all-important mouthpiece. The most effective design I've used involves shaving a short section off the back edge to allow your lips to get well behind the blowhole, then shaving a longer one off the front edge, cutting slightly into the circular through-hole to give the mouthpiece for blowing over.

Experiment with various angles and different strengths of blowing. It may seem as though your flute isn't working, and then you'll suddenly get the knack. Often a gentler blow will make it sing!

COCONUT RATTLE

This one's obvious, really. Simply cut open the coconut as carefully as you can and scoop out the flesh. Then fill it with dried beans and cover with rubber bands to hold it together.

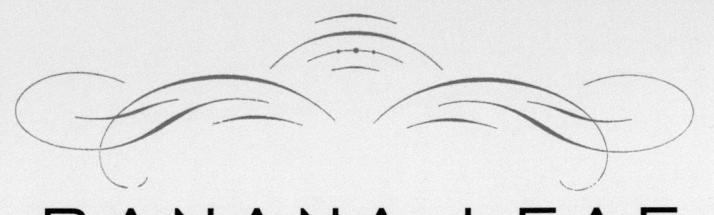

BANANA LEAF
TAKEAWAY FEAST

Oh, the sheer cheek of it. Yes, this recipe really does include one entire take-away meal for six from your local curry house. If you've got friends coming over for dinner but you're not going to get home until five minutes before they're due to arrive, this is a brilliant way to rescue an evening. If your mates are like mine, they don't mind what they eat, as long as it's served with love. So buy a bundle of banana leaves from your local Indian, Chinese or Thai shop and keep them in the fridge (they'll last for a couple of weeks), then on the day of your meal, order a takeaway meal from your favourite Indian restaurant to be delivered when you get home.

When I serve this for my friends, we all eat using our fingers, and I really urge you to try it. It's an extraordinary sensation and it makes a meal into a sensual extravaganza – I just can't recommend it enough. I have a wonderful Keralan restaurant nearby and their food is sweet, fragrant and sublimely coconutty, perfect for this leaf-based meal. When you've finished, the leaves and scrapings all go into the compost bin, so there's no washing up either. Of course, there's no point fibbing about the source of your food – that's all part of the fun!

A little while ago I made a TV series all about feasts around the world, and in Kerala I took part in the extraordinary Sadya feast as part of the Onam celebrations to welcome the mythical King Mahabali back home for his annual visit. Almost 30 million people across the state sit down to exactly the same meal at exactly the same time, regardless of their faith, wealth or social status. It's a remarkable and typically Keralan display of solidarity, and it's all eaten on a banana leaf.

SERVES 6

6 large banana leaves
a takeaway Indian meal for 6

This is traditionally eaten with everyone sitting on the floor, using their fingers. I wouldn't worry too much about the floor, but you really should try eating with your fingers.

Order around nine different dishes, wipe your banana leaves with a damp cloth before use, then put a little of each dish around the edge of each banana leaf, with a big pile of rice in the middle.

At the end of your meal, just fold up the banana leaves and throw the whole lot in the compost bin.

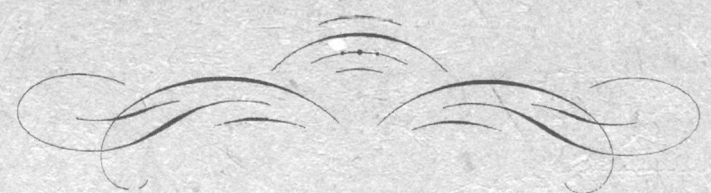

CRAB AND HAMMER PARTY

The unfettered pleasure of walloping a crab with a hammer, and hang the consequences, is what a crab-and-hammer party is all about. Maybe it's just me, but sometimes there's this exhilarating urge to cast caution and manners to the wind, grab the kitchen table, hoik it into the garden and make a huge mess of lunch. There are few ways of having more fun with your food and your friends, and this is without question my favourite way to eat – the very definition of an extraordinary meal.

Often the most spectacular feasts are the simplest, and this one is ridiculously easy. If you wanted to, you could catch the crabs yourself and boil them in a vast pan of salted water (we've done this before and it's wonderful), but nobody would hold it against you if you just buy some lovely freshly cooked crabs (and maybe a lobster, too, if you're feeling flush) from the fishmonger. (Get them the same day.) I'd urge you to make your own mayonnaise, though – it's delicious and pretty easy.

If you own enough hammers for all your guests, you are either a builder or a bit weird. Ask your friends to bring a hammer with them, perhaps some goggles (these aren't really needed, but it adds to the fun!) and maybe a shirt or apron that they don't mind getting messy. Give each of them a crab, a fork, and maybe a chopping board if you care for your table, and let the mayhem commence. You can, of course, do all of this indoors in the comfort of your own kitchen/dining room/bedsit – just try to avoid the food fight.

One medium-sized cooked crab per person
  (750g–1kg each; male or cock crabs are best – any
  larger and I'd serve one crab between two people)
plenty of mayonnaise (see page 121)
lemon wedges
crusty bread and butter and some fine ales, to serve

If you've bought live crabs, drop them in boiling water, bring back to the boil and cook for 12 minutes (up to 1kg) or 18 minutes (up to 2kg) then remove and leave to cool.

If you've bought cooked crabs, keep them in the fridge until near crabfest time. Clean your table and lay it with all the food and tools (and a chopping board if your table is posh). Give each person a little pot of mayo, a wedge of lemon and a crab, and let rip.

MAYONNAISE

A LITTLE GUIDE TO DISMANTLING A CRAB

If you need any help dismantling your crab, here are the basics. Start by pulling all the legs and claws off for individual meat-mining, then pull the entire undercarriage away from the main shell, either by yanking it out via the mouth socket or by placing the crab upended, eyes down on a board, and pushing against the leg casing until the body detaches. Discard the dead men's fingers you find inside (you'll know them when you spot them) and any stringy gills and plasticky-looking bits. If you want to help, cut each of the main body-casings in half with a large strong knife to allow access to the nuggets of flesh inside, and then set to cracking, hammering, picking, sucking and pulling, not forgetting the utterly delicious brown meat inside the main shell.

Georgia swears by making mayonnaise by hand, to the extent that I feel tangibly guilty when she catches me making it in a food-processor. She's right, too: you can taste a little sprinkling of love in handmade mayo. It really doesn't take that much longer either – probably as long as it takes to wash up a food-processor. Keep spare mayo in the fridge – it'll last for at least 2 days.

MAKES 450ML

2 large egg yolks
1 teaspoon Dijon or English mustard
salt and freshly ground black pepper
300ml sunflower oil
100ml non-virgin olive oil
zest and juice of ½ lemon
finely chopped coriander or thyme
    (optional)

HANDMADE METHOD

Put a damp cloth down and place a large mixing bowl on top (the cloth will stop the bowl from skidding around). Add the egg yolks, mustard, salt and pepper to the bowl and mix together using a whisk or wooden spoon. Now start adding the two oils in a slow drizzle, stirring all the time and making sure that it mixes to a firm fluffy mayo. When you've used up all the oil, slowly add the lemon zest and juice, continuing to whisk. Check for seasoning, and if you are adding herbs, fold them in now. Stand back and feel proud.

FOOD-PROCESSOR METHOD (SORRY, GEORGIA)

Put the egg yolks in the food-processor and add the mustard and a good pinch of salt and a grind of pepper. Whizz to mix them together, then, with the processor still running, carefully add the sunflower and olive oils in a slow trickle. The mixture should stay nice and thick and have a good yellow colour. Next gradually add the lemon zest and juice. The mayonnaise will loosen a little and turn slightly paler in colour. Check for seasoning, and if you are adding herbs, fold them in now.

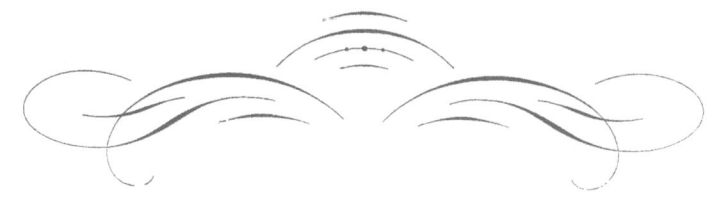

SUSHI ROLLING PARTY

Sushi-making is *brilliant*, and my mates all have a wild time whenever we make this, intoxicated by sheer culinary mayhem. I know that some people think sushi is complicated, and others are scared of serving raw fish. However, I implore you to try this out with your friends: you'll have a riot making it and you'll discover a whole culinary world that's fascinating, healthy (just use very fresh fish) and cheap, to boot. If you find it tricky making sushi for the first time, that's absolutely fine: learning alongside your friends is fun, and transforms rubbish technique into glorious failure.

It's easy to throw a sushi party. All the ingredients and equipment you need are available in big supermarkets these days, including seaweed sheets and bamboo sushi-rolling mats (these are pretty cheap, so buy a few – one mat shared between two friends is perfect). If you can't find wasabi, English mustard or (even better), fresh grated horseradish root are great substitutes.

So what preparation is needed? Well, you need to cook the sushi rice and prepare the fillings beforehand, taking good care of your salmon (see note on page 149 about freezing salmon), but a good fishmonger can prepare the fish for you. If it's your first time, I wouldn't complicate things: stick to sushi rolls using salmon, cucumber and avocado. I often put a few plates of sashimi (raw fish) around the table too (see page 147) and you'll see from the photo that strips of mackerel are also great to use. You might be surprised to find that most fish is fantastic to eat raw – my favourites are salmon, mackerel, red snapper, sea bass and butterfish.

Bear in mind that one person will need to cut the long sushi rolls into the smaller mouth-sized portions on a chopping board (I tend to do this for everyone). Make sure your very sharp knife is wiped cleaned after cutting each roll otherwise the starch left on the knife makes it a bit sticky and clumsy. If you're doing this for 12 friends – as I did last night – the cutting can keep you pretty busy, but it adds to the mayhem and fun.

The recipe here is the pared-down entry-level approach to sushi – once you're tried this, you'll probably want to spread your wings, refine your techniques and explore the wonderful world of konbu, ponzu and katsuobushi.

SERVES 6

600g sushi rice
110ml rice vinegar
5 tablespoons caster sugar (or mirin)
3 teaspoons salt
(the above 3 ingredients can be substituted for 80ml pre-seasoned sushi rice vinegar, if you've bought it)

750g very fresh wild salmon fillet, skinned and pin-boned (or 400g salmon and 3 mackerel fillets prepared as for Sashimi, see page 148)
1 red pepper
2 cucumbers
2 ripe avocados
20 nori seaweed sheets
wasabi powder (or English mustard or grated fresh horseradish root)
light soy sauce, for dipping

TO SERVE (OPTIONAL)
sake, pickled ginger and a selection of Japanese or Chinese pickled vegetables

QUAILS MAYHEM

There's a simple scientific explanation as to why quails taste so good: because they are small, they have a higher surface-to-volume ratio. This means, basically, that you get more skin per mouthful of meat, and as we all know, the skin is where the flavour is. However, unlike chickens, which tend to have a fair amount fat under the skin (which the weight-conscious of you may be wary of), the quail skin is pretty lean, with just enough fat to make it meatily and sweetly crispy but not so much that it will expand your waistline. There's also something a little extraordinary about having a whole bird to yourself.

I like to serve this with no cutlery on the table so that my friends get thoroughly finger-lickingly involved with their food. With that in mind, you'll need napkins! The trick is to wait until the birds are cool enough to touch (they need to rest anyway to be at their best), and serve them with just some nice crusty bread, or with other finger-friendly vegetables, such as small carrots and baby new potatoes.

How many quails can one person eat? Some might say that one per person is too little, but if you're eating every last morsel by gnawing the whole thing, two per person would be profligate. I used to swear that serving too much was part of the fun of a feast, but I've changed my ways when it comes to meat. Perhaps serve one per person, and give your friends lots of fantastic bread to scoff with it.

SERVES 6

6 garlic cloves, finely chopped
4 tablespoons Dijon mustard
1 tablespoon fresh thyme leaves
3 tablespoons olive oil
salt and freshly ground black pepper
6 quails
plenty of crusty bread, to serve

Mix the garlic, mustard, thyme leaves, olive oil and seasoning together in a large bowl, and mix to create a messy sauce. Roll the quails in the sauce, rubbing it into the skin using your hands, and push a little of it into the quails' cavities, too. Set aside (not in the fridge) to marinate for a little while (30 minutes would be great, but 10 minutes would be fine).

Heat a grill very hot, lay some foil over your grill pan and place the quails on it. Grill them for about 5–10 minutes until nicely browned and crispy, then turn them over and grill the other side for another 5–6 minutes. I like to serve them a little pink in the legs, but do make sure that the juices run clear (free of blood) when pricked at the thigh with a knife. Serve with loads of bread.

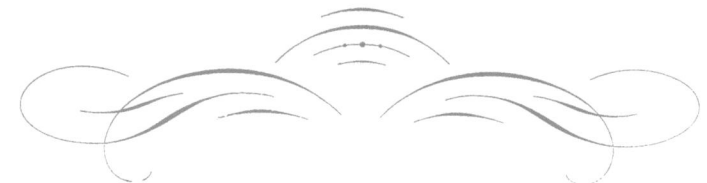

WHOLE CRISPY DUCK WITH PANCAKES

It's odd that people don't make crispy duck at home more often when it's so popular at Chinese restaurants. Perhaps it sounds unapproachably difficult to make or flamboyantly expensive, but in fact it's surprisingly easy, and for the price of one portion at a restaurant you could feed yourself and five of your friends at home – as you're mixing it with salad and pancakes, the meat goes quite a long way. I really wouldn't bother making the pancakes yourself (none of my Chinese friends would consider doing anything so time-consuming), but instead buy them frozen so that you have them to hand whenever you choose to cook the duck. It's a good idea to keep a jar of plum sauce in your cupboard, too.

I've eaten this at the legendary Quanjude restaurant in Beijing, world famous for its crispy duck. There, they bring the duck to your table on its own gurney, and a silent chef in a ridiculously tall hat cuts it into 50 separate slices. If I were you, I'd forget the hat and the 50 slices; retreat to the classic local Chinese restaurant approach and shred it using a pair of forks.

SERVES 6

1 duck, weighing 2.5–3kg
4 tablespoons honey
1 tablespoon white wine
1 tablespoon dark soy sauce (or
    2 tablespoons normal soy sauce)
200ml hoisin or plum sauce

TO SERVE

40–50 frozen Peking duck pancakes
    (sometimes sold as Mandarin
    pancakes), defrosted
1 cucumber, cored and cut into very
    thin strips about 10cm long
8 spring onions, cut lengthways into
    long thin strips
plum sauce

Remove any excess fat that can be pulled from the cavity of the duck and place it in a roasting tray that will fit in your fridge. Mix the honey, wine, soy sauce and hoisin or plum sauce together in a bowl, then pour this sauce over the duck and rub it in. Now store the duck breast-side down in the marinade and uncovered (it needs to dry out, for at least an hour, and overnight if possible) somewhere cool, and secure from interested cats!

Preheat the oven to 200°C. Roast the duck, uncovered, for 30 minutes, then reduce the heat to 180°C and roast for a further 1¼ hours. Check every now and then: the skin should be crisp and brown. Cover with some foil if it looks in danger of burning.

Warm the pancakes according to the instructions on the packet, then place them on the table. Put the shredded cucumber and spring onions onto separate plates and the plum sauce into a bowl, and place all on the table. Bring the whole duck to the table and either shred it yourself or, better still, ask one of your friends to do it, using a couple of forks. (Don't worry – you don't have to be elegant about this!) The legs are a little tricky, but persevere, as you'll need all the meat and skin to feed six of you.

To make each pancake, spread a little plum sauce on it first, add cucumber, spring onions and duck meat and skin, then roll it up and eat it.

SHABU-SHABU

Shabu-shabu is one of those meals that always seems to shine a light into my life, turning dinner into a party and making my friends lose their inhibitions. It's basically a healthy Japanese version of fondue, where you lay thin slices of fish, meat and vegetables around the table and put a large pot of boiling stock in the middle for everyone to poach their food in. The Japanese name 'shabu-shabu' refers to the sound of the food being waved from side-to-side through the water (it should be so thin that it cooks in seconds), and it's very similar to Chinese and Singaporean dishes known as steamboats. At the end of the meal you give everyone a bowl of noodles and then pour the remaining stock over for a palate-cleansing noodle soup.

I've created this slightly untraditional version using ingredients more commonly available in our supermarkets, although if you can lay your hands on a bottle of sesame dipping sauce and ponzu (a lemony soy sauce) that would be great (see Suppliers, page 218).

You could make elaborate dashi stock or homemade fish stock (the best I ever made was from old prawn shells) but there's so much fun and flavour in the cooking process that all you really need is a gentle, fragrant stock (a really good bouillon would do), and some food to dip into it (a vegetarian version would be fine, too).

ESSENTIAL KIT
In practical terms, you do need some sort of heating device in the middle of the table for this, but it doesn't need to be a fondue set – a camping stove would happily do the trick as long as it's stable. I use a very cheap tabletop portable gas burner, and they are widely available, as are the replacement gas cannisters. Actually, I have three burners for big feasts: unless you have a circular table, one pot and burner usually works only for up to six people, otherwise your friends will be sitting too far away from the pan to be able to comfortably cook.

Chopsticks are really useful for this dish, and if you really get into shabu-shabu, you can buy little basket/spoon utensils (they look a little like tea strainers) from Chinese supermarkets that are handy, although not really essential, tea strainers would do just as well.

SERVES 6

2 skinless chicken breasts, very thinly sliced
(see method)
300g pork fillet, very thinly sliced (see method)
400g beef fillet, very thinly sliced (see method)
2 litres good light chicken stock,
warmed to a simmer
1 large piece of konbu seaweed (optional)
8 Chinese cabbage leaves, washed and
thickly sliced
1 head of broccoli, cut into small florets
3 carrots, cut into long thin slices
150g spinach, washed
250g mushrooms (enoki if available),
sliced if large
350g pack firm tofu, diced
300g rice noodles, cooked according to packet
instructions, refreshed in cold water and
tossed in oil to prevent them clumping

FOR THE DIPPING SAUCE
100ml soy sauce
75g caster sugar
75ml rice vinegar
4 spring onions, finely chopped
4 egg yolks
½ medium-hot red chilli, sliced thinly
shop-bought ponzu sauce and sesame
dipping sauce (optional)

Unless you're a whizz with a knife, put your meat into the freezer for 45 minutes before slicing to help you cut it as thinly as possible. Don't worry too much about this though – the Japanese usually buy meat pre-cut to the thickness of bacon, but even chunks would be fine – really. This dish isn't about authenticity – it's about fun.

To make the dipping sauce, put all the sauce ingredients into a jam jar or bowl and stir thoroughly to combine. Divide it between small bowls or teacups so that everyone has one of their own. Give everyone a plate, a set of chopsticks, a spoon and a bowl of dipping sauce (and another of ponzu sauce or sesame dipping sauce, if using).

Place your tabletop burner or camping stove in the middle of the table, put a wide, flat pan on it (a frying-pan would do at a push), and add the stock and konbu seaweed (if using). Arrange the meat and vegetables on several plates so

that everyone can reach them. Bring the stock to a gentle simmer (skimming off any scum that might rise to the surface) and invite everyone to start cooking the meat and vegetables in the hot stock.

The meat cooks very quickly (especially if you've cut it thinly), and the beef really only needs to be waved through the simmering stock from one side to the other otherwise it gets tough and rubbery. Chicken takes a little longer, as do the vegetables. Adjust the temperature as you see fit – the more meat and veg you dip in the stock, the lower the temperature gets. Once each piece of food is cooked, it should be fished out, dipped in the dipping sauce and eaten.

When all the meat and vegetables are finished, put some cooked noodles into individual bowls, pour over the remaining flavoured stock and any stray ingredients, and serve everyone a bowl of noodle soup. They can add any remaining sauces too.

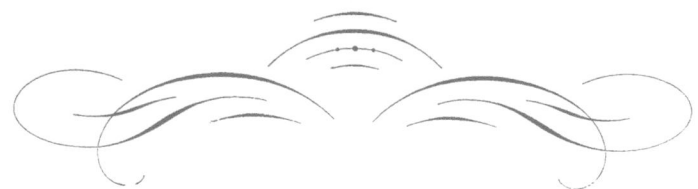

POLENTA ON THE TABLE

I do like my food to be naughty, and this is probably the naughtiest dish of all. Clear the table, give it a good wipe and then slap your polenta (or mashed potato, risotto or a whole roast dinner, for that matter) straight on top. Watch the kids' eyes light up, or your friends' mouths gape in astonishment, then hand around the forks and get everyone to dig in. I guarantee that this will be another extraordinary meal that they will never forget, and with such little effort. Let's face it: you're probably going to wipe the table down after the meal anyway, and then there's all the washing up to do. Save yourself the effort and feel the exhilaration of breaking free from convention.

If you really can't bring yourself to eat straight off the table (maybe it's like our old kitchen table, with food-catching woodworm holes that hide who-knows-what), you can still enjoy a lot of the fun by using a large chopping board or two, or perhaps a tray.

SERVES 6

1kg Cumberland sausages
1 red onion, finely chopped
2 tablespoons olive oil
500g polenta (easy-cook is fine, but the
    slow-cook version has a better texture)
250g Parmesan
salt and freshly ground black pepper
½ tablespoon flour
1 glass red wine
200ml chicken stock

Preheat the oven to 200°C. Put the sausage and chopped onion in a roasting pan that's suitable for putting on the hob later, add the oil and stir it around to coat. Roast for 20 minutes (turning after the first 10 minutes), or until golden brown and cooked through. Don't let the onions blacken – turn the heat down if necessary.

While the sausages are roasting, cook your polenta according to the instructions on the packet. When cooked through, add the Parmesan, season and stir through. Keep warm.

Remove the sausages from the roasting pan and keep warm. Tip away any excess fat from the pan then stir the flour into the onions and put the pan on the hob over a medium heat. Add the wine to the pan, stir in and let it bubble for 4 minutes, then add the stock and simmer for about 5 minutes until you have a nice thick gravy.

Spoon one or two big pools of polenta onto a clean table (or chopping boards if you can't bear to eat straight off the table), lay the sausages in the middle and pour just enough gravy over the top to lubricate it, but not to create a messy pool. Hand round the forks and encourage your friends to go for it!

6

SPECTACULAR MAINS

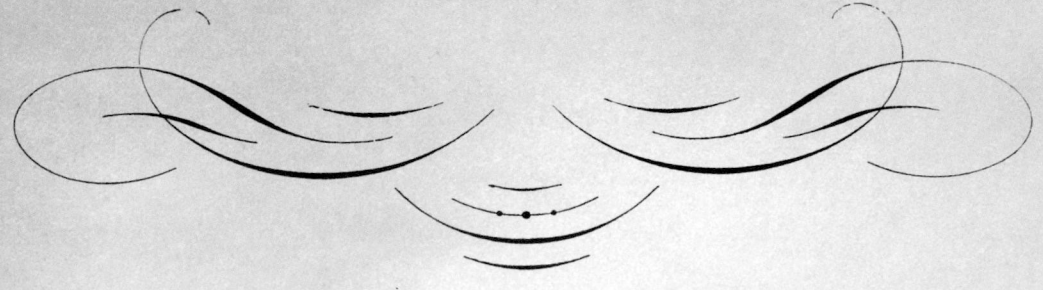

WHEN YOU'RE READY TO CREATE A MEAL that your friends will never forget, you don't need lots of money, lots of skill or even lots of food. You just need love, inspiration and the will to do something a little different. Many of the recipes in this book are ways of reinventing the eating experience to get people playing with their food and to join in the exhilaration of communal cooking, but sometimes I just feel like cooking a meal that hits the table like a sunburst. Sometimes I want my friends to feel that dinner has turned into a feast and that this is a moment that will stay in their memories forever. So I humbly offer you these spectacular dishes whose simple intention is to take your friends' breath away.

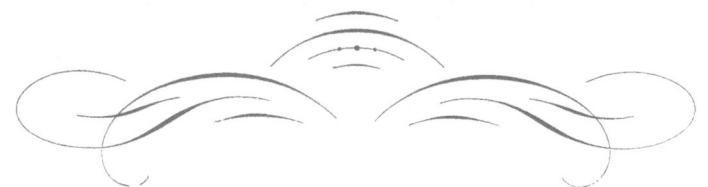

BARBECUED OYSTERS

One of the best afternoons of my life was spent trudging through the silt off Whitstable to gather oysters with my friends Anneka and Angus and our assorted kids. We pulled about 30 vast oysters out of the shingle and carried them back to their beach hut. The very largest could be opened only with a screwdriver and a hammer, but when it finally yielded, it revealed not one, but *four* pearls. Admittedly, they were little bigger than a match head, but I've eaten several thousand oysters in my life and not one has ever given me so much as a hint of rotund grit before. The wonderful element of hope that sprinkles a faint stardust over each and every one of these bivalves has been revived!

Oysters are magical little bivalves, but I know that some people are put off eating them, either because they are difficult to open or because they are squeamish about eating raw seafood. The great thing about barbecuing is that it solves both those problems in one go.

Just place your whole unopened oysters on the grill of a good, red-hot barbecue and sit back. (Be wary of putting them directly on the coals: in my experience oysters drip water out of their shells before they pop open, which can make the charcoal spit dangerously.)

In about 4–8 minutes (depending on the obstinacy of your bivalves) they will pop their lids open by a cm or two, having gently poached in their own sweet salty water. Remove from the heat as they open and allow to cool for a minute or two, then pull the upper shell right off and eat the delicious nugget that lies within.

WHOLE BAKED FISH

I know I keep saying this, but spectacular food doesn't need to be complicated, and baking a whole large fish is a perfect illustration of this. When you place a huge brill on the table, simply cooked, its skin crisp and its flesh moist and fragrant, you're likely to earn a round of applause despite a shocking lack of effort on your part. It's all in the vision rather than the work, so be bold and you'll lay on a spread fit for a king within an hour of getting home from work.

Now, you could cook a six-person John Dory or brill if your wallet can stretch to it, but no one will think any the less of you if you limit yourself to a much cheaper fish like a plaice. If you've managed to plan ahead (in which case you're infinitely more organised than me), you could order the fish to ensure that you have a whole fish of your choice that's large enough to feed your friends. Otherwise your fishmonger should be able to guide you as to how large a fish you'll need and what's best for baking from his slab.

The technique is essentially the same for all these fish, although they do take to different herbs if you fancy experimenting. The yield of John Dory is less than plaice or brill, but the intensity of its flavour seems to make up for this. I recently tried this recipe with Dover sole, and it was outrageously good.

SERVES 6

8 fresh thyme sprigs
1 tablespoon fresh rosemary leaves
olive oil
1.5kg whole fish (e.g. brill, sole plaice or
    John Dory –1 large fish if possible), gutted
    and descaled but head kept on
100g butter, cut into small chunks
salt and freshly ground black pepper
a small handful of parsley
1 lemon, cut into segments
crust bread, creamy mashed potato or sautéed
    potatoes, and some green beans, to serve

Preheat the oven to 220°C. Spread a pool of olive oil in a large, low-sided baking tray, then scatter half the herbs on it, and lay the whole fish on top, its eyes facing upwards if you're cooking a flat fish. Scatter the rest of the thyme and rosemary over the fish and dot all over with small chunks of butter. Season liberally with salt and pepper.

Bake uncovered in the oven for 20–35 minutes (this depends on the thickness of your fish) until the skin is crispy and the flesh is opaque but still moist. Remove from the oven, scatter the parsley on top and place the whole roasting tray in the middle of the table (put it on a large chopping board if that's easier) with the lemon. Let your friends dig into the fish themselves, separate the fillets from the bones, and, if necessary, spooning the juices to use as a sauce.

Serve with crusty bread, creamy mash or sautéed potatoes and some crunchy green beans.

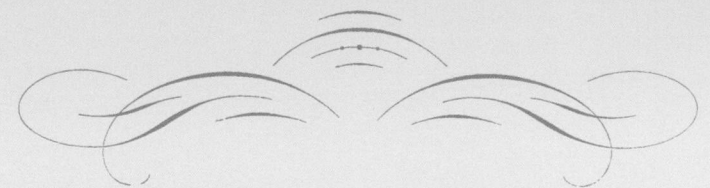

ROASTED FISH HEADS

It's well known that fish and meat stay moist and tender when cooked on the bone, and this principle is taken to its ultimate manifestation when you cook large fish heads. While the prized part of a chicken is the little 'oyster' tucked underneath the base (which I always steal when carving), the best morsel from a fish is the cheek, sat just under the skin between the eyes and gills. But all the other meat that rests against and around the head is delicious too.

This dish is very handy if you're feeling the pinch but want to lay on a spectacular spread for your friends. You can use any large fish head – I've used conger eel heads in the past, which were sublime – and the fishmonger may even give them to you for free if you're buying other fish at the same time. I often pick up a few particularly meaty heads when I spot them in the fishmonger's, then pop them in the freezer for a rainy day. If you're paying for the heads, ask the fishmonger to leave a little extra meat on the shoulders. Salmon, cod and large coley or pollack are good for this dish, and I once managed to salvage a very large John Dory head, which was excellent. The Spanish make this with hake heads, and the tongues are a great delicacy.

You'll need to use your (or your fishmonger's) best judgement as to how many heads you'll need, but as a rough guide, a small head from a fish weighing up to 2kg will serve one, a larger head from a fish weighing 2–4kg will serve two people and a whopper may be enough for four.

SERVES 6

6 medium fish heads
2 lemons, sliced
olive oil
salt and freshly ground black pepper
6 fat garlic cloves, roughly chopped
6 thyme sprigs
a handful of fresh rosemary leaves
rice or couscous and a salad, to serve
    (optional)

Preheat the oven to 220°C. Rinse the heads, pat them dry with kitchen paper, then, using a sharp knife, make a few slashes in the skin of each one. Lay half the lemon slices on a roasting tray, then lay the fish heads on top. Pour a good slug of olive oil over each head, then season with plenty of salt and pepper and half of the garlic, and rub into the skin. Push a few leaves of thyme and rosemary into each slash of the skin, pop a few in the mouth and gill-vents, and tuck any remaining ones under the fish. Scatter the remaining herbs and garlic over the top and pour some more oil over to make sure the fish heads are well lubricated.

Bake, uncovered, in the oven for 20–45 minutes, depending on the size of the heads. Serve, garnished with the remaining lemon slices, with rice or couscous and a salad.

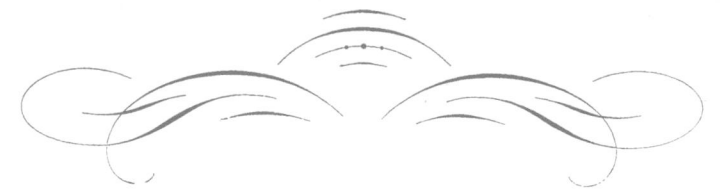

CHOCOLATE-TIN SMOKED SALMON

Hot-smoking is a rudimentary and slightly magical way to cook that's so simple you won't quite believe it works until you try it. Just a handful of hardwood shavings and a handful of herbs are enough to both cook and smoke the fish, giving it a very different, more noticeably smoky taste than the cold-smoked salmon you're familiar with, and a surprisingly delicate texture. Kids especially love the theatre of hot-smoking, and if you want to make them 'ooh' and 'aah', you can create plumes of smoke by pulling the lid off the tin while it's still on the heat. If you're being much more grown-up about the whole affair, or are in danger of tripping the smoke alarm, just let the tin cool after cooking. Despite the photo here (I got a bit carried away), you can do this in your kitchen without smoking the place out, providing you switch on the cooker hood fan.

The wood chips and herbs inside the tin start to smoulder within seconds of putting the tin over a flame and the heat cooks the fish in just 3–8 minutes (depending on the thickness of the fillet and the heat source), while the smoke swirls around in convection currents, giving it a deep smokehouse flavour. The first time you try this you'll probably be tempted to cook the salmon for longer, but trust me: test after 3 minutes and try to retain a little pinkness in the middle. If you smoke it for too long, the flavour will be overpowering.

I've used the tin in the photo for seven years now, and it's survived everything from camp fires to gas hobs - it's light, handy to carry, and it never needs more than a quick scrub out. I've added bolts as handles for the lid and base to make things easier, but you don't really need them. You can happily substitute mackerel fillets for this recipe – but bear in mind that they take even less time to cook.

KIT

a length of unpainted chicken wire, an old grill rack or a
   piece of metal mesh (mine is cut from an old
   disposable barbecue)
1 large chocolate or biscuit tin
a few large handfuls of hardwood or fruitwood chips
   (not pine or coated wood as this leaves a resinous taste).
   If in doubt, buy some from an angling shop, or see
Suppliers, page 218

SERVES 4

2 handfuls of rosemary, thyme and/or bay
   leaves – preferably on the branch
vegetable oil for brushing
800g salmon fillet (removed from the
   fridge 15 minutes before use)
salt and freshly ground black pepper

Using chicken wire or metal mesh, make a little grill shelf to fit the inside the tin, curled around so it will support a hunk of fish a few cm above the base. (You can use a bundle of chicken wire, basically, as long as the top is relatively flat.) If you want to, add crude handles to the tin using one bolt jammed into the lid and another on the side of the base (you don't *need* these but they do make life a little easier).

Scatter a handful of wood chips and herbs in the bottom of the tin, then brush the grill shelf with oil to stop the fish sticking. Season the fish, then place it on the shelf. Put the lid firmly on the tin, then place it over a high heat. (A little smoke may escape but don't worry.) Cook for 3 minutes (small fillets) then remove the tin from the heat (watch out – it will be very hot) and check if it's cooked. Cook for a further few minutes if necessary, adding more wood chips as needed, but don't overcook, as the whole beauty of the dish is its moist delicacy contrasted with its strong flavour.

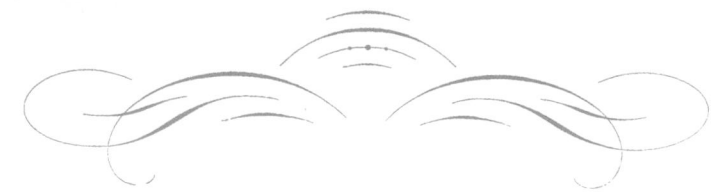

LUNCH COOKED
IN THE DISHWASHER

Yes, you really can poach salmon – and the rest of your lunch – in a dishwasher and, no, it doesn't end up tasting of soap! Dishwashers heat their water during the cycle and that heat is enough to poach salmon, and gently infuse it with the flavours of aromatic herbs. My dishwasher runs a 55–65°C cycle that makes the most meltingly delicious poached salmon, and also makes extraordinary asparagus that's very crunchy, yet oddly tender too. The trick is to keep your fish tightly wrapped in foil, don't use detergent and run the dishwasher on the highest and hottest cycle.

You don't have to use an empty dishwasher, but neither would I put anything particularly dirty in it in case of contamination. By the way, other household appliances that can be employed to cook food – provided you use them with caution – are hairdryers (good for cooking pizza, though it takes a long time), steel log-burner bins (make great pizza ovens), security lamps (you can just about cook pancakes on them) and irons (great for cooking bacon).

SERVES 6

FOR THE SALMON PARCEL
1kg salmon fillet, skinned and pin-boned
olive oil
zest and juice of 2 fresh limes
a large thumb of ginger, peeled and
    thinly sliced into rounds
a large handful of coriander, finely chopped
salt and freshly ground black pepper

FOR THE ASPARAGUS PARCEL
1 bunch of asparagus
a knob of butter
salt and freshly ground black pepper

FOR THE NOODLE PARCEL
1 pack of fresh noodles
2 spring onions, finely sliced

1 teaspoon toasted sesame oil
1 teaspoon Thai fish sauce (nam pla)

FOR THE TWO MIXED VEG PARCELS
1 red pepper, cored, deseeded and
    finely sliced
500g bean sprouts
1 teaspoon toasted sesame oil
300g bok choy (Chinese cabbage),
    chopped into thick slices
a few thin slices of mild red chilli
1 tablespoon soy sauce

Place five double layers of foil, each 75cm square, on the work surface. Drizzle some oil onto each square of foil and spread it over the surface using a pastry brush.

Put the salmon fillet in the middle of one square and fold up the edges of the foil a little to make a bowl. Sprinkle over the lime zest and juice, place the ginger slices on top, then scatter the coriander on top and season. Bring the sides of the foil together, pinching to make a watertight package.

Follow the same method for the asparagus and noodle parcels, and divide the veg between two parcels, ensuring that the parcels are flat rather than round, otherwise the heat won't get to the food for long enough. Place your packages on the top rack of the dishwasher, choose the hottest and longest cycle (the parcels should cook for about 1 hour), and don't add any detergent!

At the end of the cycle, remove the parcels. Unwrap the parcels at the table and let everyone dig in.

RICE

First cook your rice as it will need time to cool a little before eating. Place it in a sieve, rinse with cold water until the water runs clear, then transfer to a large saucepan with 750ml cold water. Bring to the boil, stir and turn the heat down. Keep it boiling for 5 minutes with the lid on (making sure it doesn't boil over), then reduce the heat and simmer for a further 10 minutes stirring so that it doesn't stick and burn. Turn the heat off and leave the rice in the covered pan for a further 10 minutes. It should be lightly sticky but not soggy.

Meanwhile, mix together the rice seasonings – the vinegar, caster sugar and salt – and stir until the sugar has dissolved. Add the mixture to the cooked rice and gently stir through so the rice is shiny and sticky. Tip it into a wide bowl, then leave to cool for at least 30 minutes – it's best served at room temperature (if you can wait that long). Once it's at room temperature, you can cover the bowl with a tea towel. The rice can be served on the table in two or three separate bowls for easy access.

MACKEREL

Combine the salt, sugar and rice vinegar for the marinade in a bowl and stir until the salt and sugar have dissolved. Tightly pack the mackerel fillets into a shallow, flat, non-metallic dish, then pour over the vinegar mixture. Leave to marinate for at least 30–45 minutes (but no longer otherwise they'll overmarinate) while you prepare the rest of your fish (see below).

Remove the mackerel fillets from the vinegar and thoroughly pat dry with kitchen paper (but don't rinse). Gently pull the pin bones out with a pair of tweezers or clean pliers (this is the most fiddly bit) and then peel off the thin clingfilm-like skin layer with your fingers, starting from the head end. (You probably won't have noticed this layer before, but it sits on top of the shiny skin.) Lay the fillets shiny side up and slice into generous, finger-thick pieces. Arrange these as artfully as you fancy on a board or plate for serving.

SALMON

Ah, the easy bit. Rinse it in cold water then pat dry. Trim the underside of the fillet to remove any grey or dark red-coloured flesh next to the skin (this is only for appearance, so don't worry if you find it too difficult). Lay the fillet flat on a board and cut short, fat, finger-width slices and arrange them artfully on a board or plate.

SCALLOPS

Ah, even easier! Rinse them in cold water then pat dry. Remove and reserve the orange roes, pull off the tough little knob of meat from the side, along with the membrane wrapped around the scallop. Carefully cut each scallop into three or four 3mm-thick slices and arrange them with the roes on a board or plate.

SQUID

The fishmonger should have removed any membranes, but double-check. Cut across the main body to create thin rings, then arrange the legs on a plate and lay out the rings around it.

WASABI OR HORSERADISH

Mix the wasabi powder with just enough water to form a thick paste, then leave it to rest for 5 minutes. Mould the wasabi paste into lumps and divide between the plates of fish. If you're using horseradish root, simply grate it finely and use in the same way as the prepared wasabi.

TO SERVE

Serve all the sashimi, wasabi and rice at the same time, on separate plates, giving each of your friends a plate, chopsticks and a little bowl of soy sauce (use teacups if you don't have enough). The wasabi is for dabbing on each piece of fish, if desired. Sake is a perfect accompaniment, naturally.

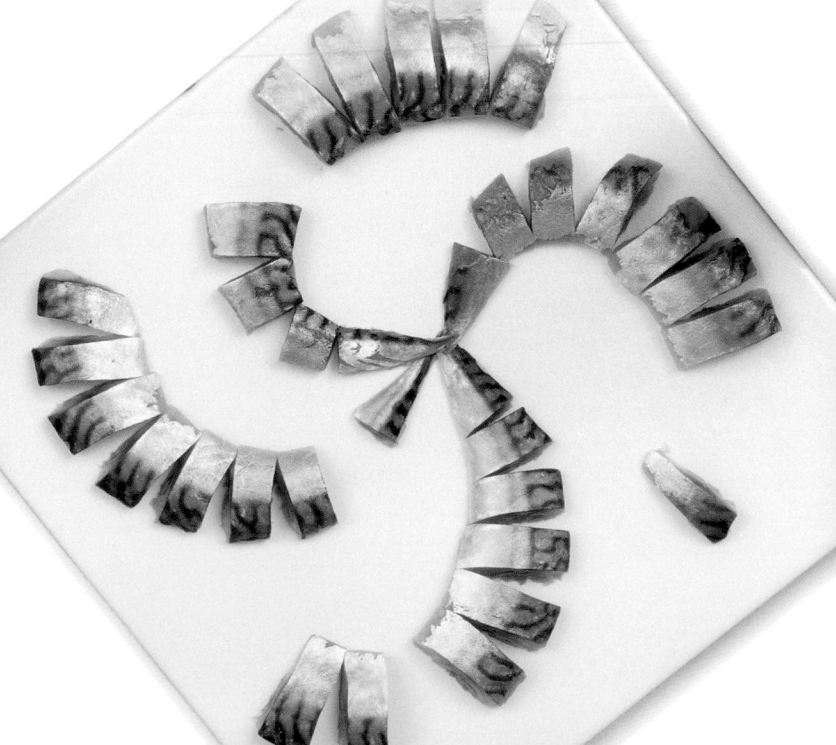

A NOTE ABOUT RAW FISH

Should you freeze fish before eating it raw? The UK Food Standards Agency recommends that fish for commercial sushi and sashimi should be frozen to −20°C (the temperature of most domestic freezers) for at least 24 hours before use to kill parasites that may be in the fish. This is good advice, but I must say that I don't freeze any of my fish as long as I trust my source, and chefs in Japan don't either (although arguably they have better handling standards in Japan because so much fish there is destined for sushi). The most important thing is to use very fresh fish from a supplier you trust, and mention to them that you'll be eating it raw – your fishmonger will probably give you the very best fish he or she has!

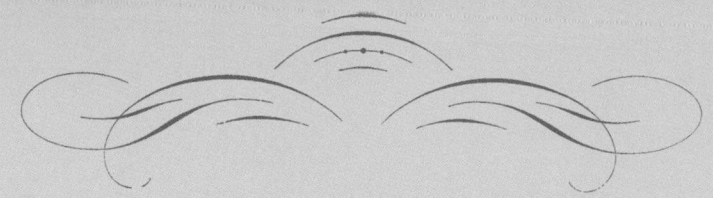

HERBY SALT-CRUST BAKED CHICKEN

This recipe has magic and drama in spades. It's amazing to see a whole chicken arrive at the table encased in an armour of herby salt and to smell the intensity of the flavours as they burst forth when you crack it open. The salt crust acts as a seal, keeping the flavourings close to the skin as the chicken steams within. You'll need to throw all the salt away once the bird is cooked – and do be careful as you crack the crust open so the salt doesn't mix too much with the meat. Bear in mind that you won't get any useable juices from the chicken when it's cooked in this way.

SERVES 4

1.5kg free-range chicken
1kg coarse salt or rock salt
1 lemon, zested, juiced and husks reserved
a large handful of rosemary leaves, chopped
1 tablespoon thyme leaves
4 garlic cloves, thinly sliced
4 bay leaves

Preheat the oven to 200°C. Rinse the chicken, but leave it trussed, and pat dry. In a large bowl, mix the salt together with the lemon zest and juice and half the rosemary, thyme and garlic. Add just enough water to make it damp – it should have the consistency of seaside-castle-building sand.

Push the lemon husks into the chicken cavity, ensuring that you close it up afterwards. Line a roasting tin with foil, then lay a bed of salt, using about a quarter of what's in your bowl, over its base. Place the bay leaves on the salt, then put the chicken on top. Scatter the remaining herbs and garlic on top of the chicken, and then pack the rest of the salt around it until it's well covered. Cover the whole lot with another layer of foil.

Bake for 1½ hours, then remove the tin from the oven and carefully peel back the foil. Bring the tin to the table and break open the salt crust to reveal the chicken inside. Break off and discard all the salt, then carve the chicken and serve with potatoes and vegetables and perhaps a lemony/garlicky gravy.

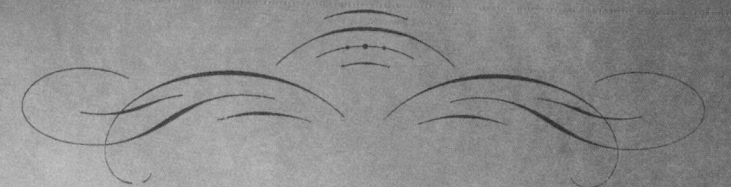

GOLDEN CHICKEN

One thing is certain: if you cook golden chicken for your friends, they will never, ever forget it. You'll also be pleasantly surprised to find that it's easy to make and not as expensive as you might think. I've been gilding food for years – mostly sausages and chocolates for the sheer excitement they cause, especially for kids. The difference with this gilded chicken is not just the extraordinary spectacle but also its taste, because it just so happens that the best cooking method for chicken-gilding is also an absurdly easy way to make the moistest, most tender chicken imaginable, using the simple *poule au pot* method of gently poaching the chicken together with some vegetables. You can make this in advance and keep (or reheat) it in the oven to retain the element of surprise.

I'd be crazy to ignore the glaringly profligate, materialistic symbolism of eating gold, so it's only right that I offer you some ideas for justifying your extravagance to your guests, should you feel the need to do so. The first justification is that gold leaf is so thin that only a microscopic amount is needed to gild a whole chicken, costing perhaps half the price of a bottle of Champagne. And hey, you're not going to eat gold every day – that would be tacky. Secondly, this is celebration food with an ancient pedigree that often features at Indian weddings and on sweets and chocolates. Your third justification is simply this: 'Oh my God, look! It's a golden chicken! Oh my God!'

GOLD LEAF
Gold is odourless and tasteless, and gold leaf has been beaten to the thickness of a few atoms, which means that it doesn't react on metal fillings like aluminium foil does. It's safe to eat – it's a permitted food additive with its own E number (E175 – silver is E174).

You can buy gold leaf in booklets from either art suppliers or edible decoration suppliers, but I'd shop around as the prices vary wildly (art suppliers are invariably cheaper). Check how many leaves are in the book and what size they are. You're looking for transfer leaf of at least 23 carat purity, which comes in books of 25 leaves, each pressed against a leaf of tissue paper. Loose leaf is a little trickier to handle, and gold powder is extremely expensive.

1.5kg free-range chicken
1 medium onion, peeled and halved
bouquet garni made from 5 flat-leaf
    parsley stalks, 3 thyme sprigs and
    3 bay leaves, tied together with string
500ml chicken stock (fresh or made
    with a chicken stock cube)
salt and freshly ground black pepper
500g small new potatoes, scrubbed
500g medium carrots, scrubbed but
    kept whole
a handful of baby onions, peeled
small turnips or chopped parsnips
    (optional)
about 12 leaves of parchment gold
    from a book of 25 leaves
broccoli or peas, to serve

If your chicken is trussed, keep it like that to retain its shape. Pop the halved onion into the breast cavity, and put the chicken in a saucepan or casserole large enough to fit the veg in, too. Add cold water until the chicken is completely submerged, then add the bouquet garni and stock cube and season with salt and pepper. Place the pan over a medium heat and bring slowly to a simmer.

Skim and dispose of any mucky stuff that rises to the surface, then put the lid on the pan and lower the heat. Simmer gently for 35 minutes, then add the potatoes and carrots – plus the baby onions, turnips and parsnips, if using – and simmer for a further 15 minutes.

Remove the chicken to a carving dish and test that it's cooked (the juices in the thigh should run clear when pricked with a skewer). Cover and leave to rest for 10 minutes.

Check the vegetables for tenderness and cook for a few more minutes if necessary, otherwise remove them from the stock to serving dishes, toss them in butter, season to taste and keep warm. Pour away all but 500ml of the liquid from the pan, then return the pan to the heat and reduce by about half to use as gravy.

Now for the gilding. Wipe excess moisture from the chicken with kitchen paper (although the skin will need to remain a little damp and tacky for the gold to stick) then simply press the gold transfer leaf against the chicken. The gold should come off and stick to the skin. If you need to remoisten the skin, dab it with a little of the cooking liquid, using kitchen paper or a pastry brush. You can use a small paintbrush to help fix the gold leaf in place, but avoid handling it or it will come off onto your fingers. It's fiddly, but fun! When you've finished, you can keep the chicken warm in the oven, covered with a dome of foil or another roasting dish sat upside-down, but try not to let anything touch the gold.

Cook some broccoli or peas to accompany the chicken. When you are ready to serve, put the gravy into a jug, arrange the gilded bird on the middle of a platter and surround it with the vegetables, then bring it to the table with a confused look on your face.

VARIATIONS
This is a brilliant way to cook chicken, whether you gild it or not. You could also try using pure silver leaf, too, which is a quarter of the price of gold… although this might be missing a trick.

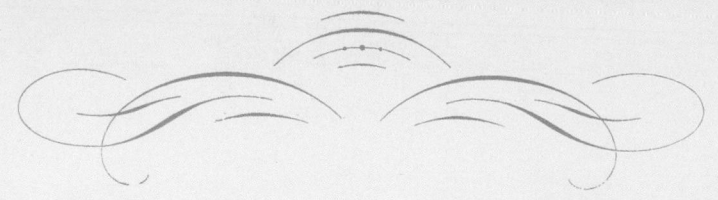

RABBIT IN CREAMY MUSTARD SAUCE

The British are extremely sentimental about rabbits so there's always an element of spectacle when they arrive at a table in the form of lunch, but across most of Continental Europe rabbit is a highly prized dish, and fetches a good price in the butchers. The reason for this contrast in attitudes is unclear – French kids love a cuddly *lapin* as much as do English ones. I think it's all down to Beatrix Potter, who so thoroughly anthropomorphised the rabbit that eating one is a bit like eating your childhood sweetheart. But whatever the reason, the result is that Brits eat few rabbits now, so fewer are hunted and they are left to party on the juicy crops of this pleasant land.

Rabbits have little fat on them, so they are a healthy meat if you're feeling fulsome, (although this also means they can dry out if overcooked); they taste like slightly gamey chicken; they are cheap, and they have an unfamiliar bone structure if you're used to carving chicken, with quite a few little bones. If you can get your hands on enough rabbit livers, they also make an excellent variation on the chicken liver parfait on page 54. Oh, and this recipe is also fantastic with chicken.

SERVES 6

10 garlic cloves, roughly chopped
4 tablespoons Dijon mustard
2 tablespoons fresh thyme leaves
8 bay leaves
salt and freshly ground black pepper
5 tablespoons olive oil
2 rabbits, each jointed into 4 legs and 3 or 4 sections of saddle (see picture, left)
2 onions, finely sliced
300ml double cream
100ml white wine or chicken stock
1 teaspoon sugar

Preheat your oven to 190°C. In a small bowl, mix together the garlic, mustard, thyme, bay leaves, salt and pepper, and 3 tablespoons of the olive oil. Rub this pungent mixture all over your rabbit pieces and lay them in a roasting tin. Bake uncovered for 25 minutes.

Meanwhile, put a frying pan over a low/medium heat and add 2 tablespoons of olive oil and the onion. Fry gently until softened and translucent, then add the cream, wine or stock and sugar to the pan and warm gently over a low heat. Remove the rabbit from the oven, stir the sauce and pour over the rabbit, making sure it's thoroughly coated, then return the tin to the oven for a further 20 minutes.

Serve the rabbit with the sauce and some boiled potatoes, or if you're feeling fancy, a parsnip or celeriac gratin.

TURDUCKEN

It's a rubbish name for an extraordinary dish. The name 'turducken' is a combination of **tur**key, **duck** and chi**cken**. (I've been trying to come up with a new name but all I've got to offer is 'turkchickuck', which is, let's face it, worse.) The dish is a poultry Russian doll, offering a chicken stuffed inside a duck, stuffed inside a turkey. I usually make one of these around Christmas or New Year, when I go to town by using as many different birds as I can manage. The most elaborate version I've managed so far was an eight-bird roast of turkey stuffed with a goose, stuffed with a capon, chicken, guinea fowl, woodcock, quail and pigeon breast – inside of which was a little chipolata.

The trick is to entirely bone the birds so that you've got one large hunk of meat. You make up for the lack of crispy skin on the inner birds by including a layer of something else – I like to add thinly sliced fruit and herbs – then when you cut it open you get a Swiss roll effect.

You can buy ready-boned and rolled turduckens all set for the oven, but I think that you might feel undeserving of the applause at the table. It's fun to do it all yourself, although there are a couple of slightly tricky stages that I'll point out now to avoid disappointment halfway through. When you bone the turkey, you need to cut the meat away from the bones very carefully so that the skin remains intact – at least over the main bulk of the breast where it touches the breastbone – and this is sometimes fiddly. This will take time, possibly an hour or more depending on your knife skills, and it's best not to rush it. You'll need to sew up the whole turducken once you've rolled it up, and although I've done this a few times with a sharp knife and some string, it's much easier to use a trussing needle (just a big needle, really) and trussing string, both of which are readily available in cookware shops. I should also point out that this is a slow-cooked dish, which will need several hours in the oven. Don't let that put you off, now!

SERVES ABOUT 14–16

5kg turkey
2.5kg duck
1.2kg chicken
salt and freshly ground black pepper
fresh thyme leaves
2 oranges, peeled and thinly sliced
2 lemons, peeled and thinly sliced
olive oil
a splash of white wine
roast potatoes, roast parsnips, buttered
carrots, buttered cabbage or greens and
cranberry sauce, to serve

Bone all the birds, taking your time so that you don't cut through the skin accidentally: using a sharp, thin knife, cut the skin along the backbone first, and then ease the skin away from the chest cavity using lots of little cuts, following the bones until you get to the legs, then cut into the meat and separate the socket from the main carcass. Leave the leg bones in for the moment, and concentrate on cutting the meat away from the carcass, continuing with those little cuts. Be very careful at the top of the breast where the skin is all that keeps it together – this is where you need to be really careful not to slice the skin. Now do the other side.

Boning the legs is a bit fiddly (you can leave them in if you don't feel confident): you'll need to scrape the flesh away from the bone bit by bit, working your way down and turning it inside out until you get to the end. Push the meat back into the skin. Unless you're really in the groove of it,

I suggest that you chop off the drumsticks and wings if they are simply too much effort. (This will obviously leave a little slit in the skin, but it's not a problem.) Continue until you've boned all three birds.

Preheat the oven to 180°C. Now, place the turkey skin-side down, season with salt and pepper, scatter over a few thyme leaves and lay some orange and lemon slices on the meat. Place the duck on top of that and repeat the layer of seasoning, thyme and orange and lemon slices, then place the chicken on top. Add a couple of orange and lemon slices in the middle.

Now you need to truss the stuffed birds into as neat a 'rugby ball' as you can. This is best done by rolling up the birds and sewing up the turkey using a trussing needle and twine. Unless you really want to keep it as a surprise, I'd suggest that you enlist the help of a friend at this stage.

Brush the turducken with olive oil and season with salt and pepper, then carefully massage the oil into the skin (this will help to stop the skin splitting). Place the turducken, breast-side down, in a roasting tin, add a splash of white wine, then cover it with foil. Roast for about 2½ hours, basting every 30 minutes or so (this helps to ensure the skin doesn't split, which can sometimes happen), and each time removing and reserving all but a few tablespoons of excess juices, (often, there's *lots* of juice!) Remove the foil and roast for a further 30 minutes. Check that the turducken is cooked by inserting a knife into a thick part of it; the juices should run clear. Cook for a little longer if need be, but be careful not to overcook it or it will be very dry.

Remove the turducken from the oven. Re-cover it with foil and leave it in the tin with some of the juices to rest for 30 minutes while you make some gravy. Put the reserved cooking juices in a saucepan and reduce by half, adding a little flour to thicken if you prefer thick gravy.

Carve, giving each person a section through the birds. Serve with roast potatoes, roast parsnips, buttered carrots, buttered cabbage or greens, gravy and cranberry sauce.

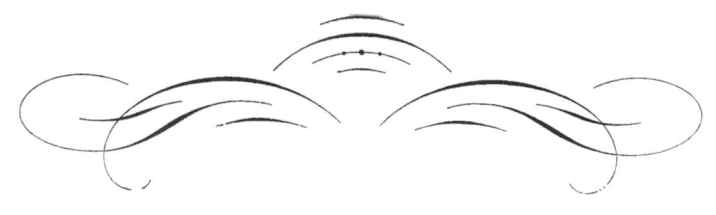

ROAST PARTRIDGE

Come autumn, my local butcher's shop begins to overflow with all manner of beautiful fresh birds: partridge, pheasant, grouse and woodcock – the names alone make me salivate. They are more expensive than average supermarket chicken, to be sure, but these birds have led a totally free-range life, and I swear you can taste it in the flesh. Some gourmands I know say that a roasted grouse, hung for a long time until the flesh is strong and heady, is their favourite food of all time. I'm not sure I'd agree, but then I've never been game shooting. I can imagine that if hunting's your bag, and you've shot a grouse yourself while standing beside a panting, wet dog in the pouring rain on some heather-covered hillside with a roaring fire waiting for you back home, the romance of it all transforms the eating experience.

If the taste of an aged grouse is too much for your palate, a great way of enjoying this season of carnivorous plenty is to eat partridge, with its milder gamey flavours and sweetness of flesh. It's not difficult to cook (unlike pheasant, which can be dry and tricky to do justice to), as long as you wrap up the bird in a nice cocoon of bacon to keep it moist.

SERVES 6

6 partridges, ready for roasting
100g butter, at room temperature
12 rashers streaky bacon
1 tablespoon plain flour
1 glass red wine
200ml chicken stock
1 tablespoon redcurrant or blackberry jelly
4 thyme sprigs
mashed potatoes or polenta and green
beans or spring greens, to serve

Preheat the oven to 200°C. Spread a little butter over each bird, then wrap each one in a couple of rashers of bacon, securing them with cocktail sticks.

Place the partridges in a roasting tin and roast uncovered for about 20 minutes, then remove the bacon (it should be nice and crispy) to a plate, cover and keep warm. Return the partridges to the oven and continue to roast for a further 10 minutes.

Remove the birds from the roasting tin, cover and keep warm. Add the flour to the roasting tin and stir it into the juices. Add the wine, stock, redcurrant jelly and thyme and let this gravy reduce to your preferred consistency.

Serve one partridge per person with the bacon, potatoes or polenta, and green beans, spring greens or other green and crunchy vegetables.

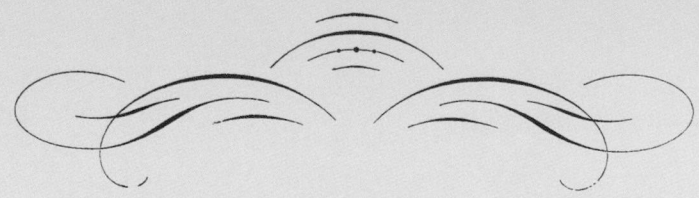

HAGGIS WITH WHISKY, TATTIES AND NEEPS

I could have given you the recipe for making haggis from scratch. The cooking process is certainly an extraordinary affair, involving the procuring of a fresh sheep's pluck (all the innards that have been 'plucked' out of the belly, including the liver, heart, lungs and windpipe) together with suet, onions, herbs and oatmeal, all stuffed in a nice, fresh stomach bag. But although I'm confident in your abilities, I'd be deluded if I really thought you'd bother.* Instead, I'll assume that you've bought a cooked and ready-to-reheat haggis from the shops (which is ambitious enough) and you'd like to know what to do with it.

Haggis tastes hearty and wholesome – as long as you don't get obsessed with the relative oddness of what's in it – and is also an excellent source of protein. I've eaten it several times in Edinburgh with a slug of whisky poured over the top, and this certainly adds an extra depth.

SERVES 6

1kg cooked, ready-to-reheat haggis
1kg turnips, peeled and quartered
250g butter
1 thumb-sized piece of fresh root
    ginger, grated
1kg potatoes, peeled and quartered
a handful of chopped chives
½ teaspoon grated nutmeg
good blended whisky

* If I'm underestimating your ambition, and you really would like to have a go, I recommend you get hold of a copy of Catherine Brown's *Scottish Cookery* (Mercat Press, Edinburgh, 2006).

Bring a large pan of water to the boil and then turn off the heat. Unless it has instructions telling you differently, remove any outer plastic packaging from the haggis, then lower it gently into the pan (you don't want it to burst). Turn on the heat again and bring it up to a very gentle simmer so that the haggis poaches all the way through. It will take about 1¼ hours to thoroughly reheat a 1kg haggis, less if the haggis is smaller.

Meanwhile, boil the turnips for 25 minutes, or until tender, then season and mash together with half the butter and the grated ginger.

Boil the potatoes for 15–20 minutes until tender, then season and mash together with the remainder of the butter, the chives and the nutmeg.

Cut open the haggis and divide between plates, with side servings of potatoes and turnips, then pour a small splash of whisky (no more, otherwise it will taste murky) on each serving of haggis. Serve with more whisky for drinking.

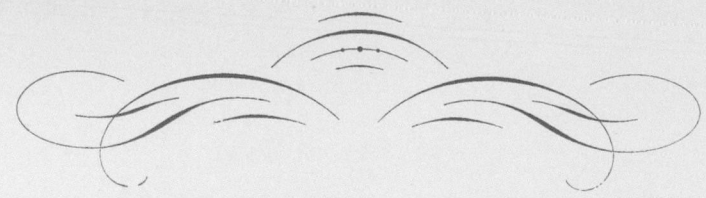

CHOCOLATE-ROASTED SPARE RIBS

I once saw a man – I kid you not – eating spare ribs with a knife and fork. I nearly asked him if he was paying penance for some unspeakable sin, but then I remembered that there's a generation for whom touching food with fingers is simply out of the question. Thankfully those days are over, and we can now revel in the laying on of hands. Ribs (and rib sauce fingers) were made for slurping, licking, sucking and generally slobbering over, and these chocolatey ones make them almost unbearably delicious. Just leave the cutlery in the drawer.

This chocolate marinade gives the ribs a rich, smoky flavour that everyone seems to love. You might be tempted to use more chocolate than the recipe suggests, but resist! Too much will make this dish cloying.

SERVES 6

1.5kg pork ribs, skin removed, cut into separate ribs

FOR THE MARINADE
150g tomato purée
100g dark chocolate, grated
1 mild red chilli, finely chopped (or
    1 teaspoon red chilli flakes)
3cm thumb of ginger, peeled and grated
1 teaspoon Chinese five-spice powder (optional)
2 tablespoons vegetable oil
2 tablespoons honey
salt and freshly ground black pepper
rice and stir-fried cabbage tossed in
    toasted sesame oil, to serve (optional)

Preheat the oven to 200°C (or better still, get your barbecue going). Place all the marinade ingredients into a saucepan and simmer over a medium heat for 2 minutes, stirring to prevent the marinade from burning.

Lay the ribs in one or two roasting trays, not too tightly packed (they can sometimes release a fair amount of moisture and you want them to roast, not poach, otherwise they can turn out a little rubbery).

Pour over the sauce and stir to ensure that the ribs are thoroughly coated. Roast uncovered in the oven for about 20–30 minutes, turning once. Check that ribs are cooked through, then serve with rice and sesame stir-fried cabbage.

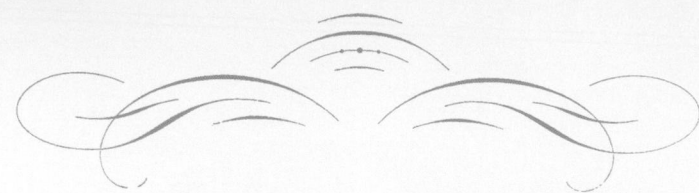

THE BIGGEST SCOTCH EGG IN THE WORLD

Oh, the sheer, joyous extraordinariness! You can buy fresh ostrich eggs from ostrich farms and posh food delis, and they aren't as expensive as you might think. In fact, when you consider that one ostrich egg is roughly equivalent to 27 hens' eggs, it doesn't actually cost *that* much more weight-for-weight. Not that economic value is of any consequence here – it's all about the spectacle.

The tricky part is getting the sausagemeat to stick to the egg evenly (my last one looked like a rugby ball). And, of course, you'll need either a large deep pan for deep-frying, or a deep-fat fryer that will cope with the scotch egg plus a couple of centimetres either side for the casing – that's a width of about 14–20cm depending on the size of the egg. The process is the same as for making a normal scotch egg: boil the egg, remove the thick shell (using a combination of hammer and fingers), cover it in sausagemeat then breadcrumbs and then cook it a second time. Finally, you'll need to get a lot of friends together for a picnic!

Serves at least 10

1 fresh ostrich egg (see Suppliers, page 218)
1.25kg good-quality sausagemeat
3 hens' eggs, beaten
400g breadcrumbs
6 litres vegetable oil, for frying

First, boil your ostrich egg for 1½ hours, then place in cold water and leave to cool until handleable.

Put the ostrich egg in a bowl to steady it, and break off the shell. You may need a hammer to crack it, but once you're in, it's pretty easy. Dry the surface of the egg thoroughly (otherwise the sausagemeat won't stick) and set it aside to cool completely. (If it's warm, the sausagemeat will go greasy and slide off).

Lightly flour a work surface and on it, spread your sausagemeat. Paint a light coating of beaten egg all over the ostrich egg using a pastry brush, and let it dry until tacky (this is to provide a good sticky surface for the sausagemeat to adhere to). Now place the egg on top of the sausagemeat, flour your hands and cover the whole egg in a thick coating of meat, pressing the sausagemeat into the egg and trying to keep it as uniform as you can (there's no ideal way of doing this, but keeping your hands well floured will help.)

Spread out the breadcrumbs on a large tray. Brush the sausagemeat-covered egg with the remainder of the beaten egg, then roll it very carefully in the breadcrumbs.

Heat the oil in a large deep pan or deep-fat fryer until very hot, then very carefully place the ostrich egg in it (I use two large slotted serving spoons). Deep-fry the egg for about 10–15 minutes, depending on the thickness of the meat, until golden brown.

Now you're ready to serve it. Make sure your friends see the whole egg before you cut into it so they know what's in store. There's no standard method for this – I like cutting it in half then into slices. Eat it as part of a picnic with boiled potatoes, salad and crisps.

CLASSIC BRAISED OXTAIL

Here's a stripped-down haute cuisine recipe for a ridiculously unctuous dish from a ridiculously cheap cut of meat. This might look overly simple, but you really don't need to complicate it – it works beautifully just as it is. As with most cheap beef cuts, the longer and more gently you cook oxtail, the more spectacular it will taste.

SERVES 6

12 large sections of oxtail
2 tablespoons plain flour
2 tablespoons vegetable oil
2 large onions, finely chopped
2 sticks celery, finely chopped
3 large parsnips, peeled and chopped
3 large carrots, peeled and chopped
1 bottle of red wine
1 tin of chopped plum tomatoes
a handful of parsley, handful of thyme and
    4 bay leaves, tied together with string
1 teaspoon chilli flakes (or ½ teaspoon
    chilli powder)
salt and freshly ground black pepper
buttery creamed potatoes, to serve

Preheat the oven to 150°C. Toss the oxtail pieces in the flour. Put a large casserole dish (one with a lid) over a high heat, add the oil and fry the oxtail pieces a few at a time until brown all over. Remove with a slotted spoon and set aside, then add the onions, celery, parsnips and carrots and fry over a medium heat until they start to brown. Add all the remaining ingredients, stir and bring to a simmer. Cover the casserole with its lid and place in the oven for 3–4 hours, checking every now and then to make sure it hasn't dried out.

Remove the casserole from the oven, then carefully transfer the oxtail pieces to a plate and keep warm. Place the casserole over a medium heat and reduce the sauce until it's nice and sticky. Serve the oxtail covered in the sauce, on a bed of buttery creamed potatoes.

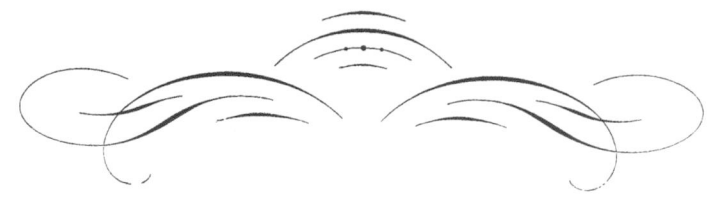

BRAISED LAMBS' HEARTS WITH GREMOLATA

Simple, delicious and extremely cheap, this slow-cooked dish tastes, oddly enough, like a very tender beef stew and has the texture of beef fillet. Six lambs' hearts cost less than my Sunday newspaper, so it's strange they aren't eaten more often. The idea of eating hearts may be off-putting for some, but these are so good that if any dish were to convince you to eat more offal, it's this one.

Of course, gremolata spreads a little joy over anything it touches – it's an amazing Italian mixture of herbs, garlic and lemon zest, which, added to any stew after it's been cooked, turns a simple, hearty dish into an explosion of flavour.

SERVES 6

6 lambs' hearts
2 tablespoons plain flour
3 tablespoons vegetable or non-virgin
    olive oil
800g root vegetables (e.g. a mixture of
    parsnips, carrots and Jerusalem artichokes),
    chopped into large chunks
salt and freshly ground black pepper
2 glasses red wine
800ml good chicken stock
400g small potatoes (peeled or not –
    it's up to you)
8 garlic cloves, roughly chopped
4 bay leaves
bouquet garni of parsley and thyme
    stalks tied together with string

FOR THE GREMOLATA
grated zest of 2 lemons
2 tablespoons lemon juice
3 garlic cloves, finely chopped
a handful of finely chopped fresh
    thyme, rosemary and parsley

The hearts need little preparation: simply cut out the tube/ventricle ends, which descend a couple of centimetres into the top of the heart. Don't worry about making a smart job of it and don't cut off the little layers of fat that sit around the top – it's fabulous stuff and helps to moisten the dish.

Spread out the flour on a plate and roll the hearts around in it to coat them thoroughly. Take a heavy-based casserole (or any good pan with a lid), add the oil and brown the hearts in two batches over a high heat for about 6–8 minutes, turning to sear them all around. Remove the hearts and set aside, then add the root vegetables (but not the potatoes) to the pan and fry for 10 minutes.

Season with salt and pepper and add the wine, stock, potatoes, garlic, bay leaves and bouquet garni to the pan. Increase the heat until the liquid starts to simmer, then put the lid on the pan and reduce the heat to as low as possible, using a heat diffuser if you have one, so that the liquid just shudders gently. Simmer for 2–4 hours (you can also do this in the oven set to 110°C if you'd rather), checking every now and then to make sure it isn't drying out and adding water if necessary.

Meanwhile, make the gremolata by stirring together the lemon zest and juice, garlic and herbs in a bowl. Set aside.

Uncover the pan and remove and discard the bouquet garni. Using a slotted spoon, decant the meat and vegetables to a large bowl, leaving all the juices behind. Boil the juices for about 5–10 minutes, or until they have reduced to a good thick gravy. Serve the hearts, vegetables and gravy in wide bowls, scattering the gremolata over each one just before serving.

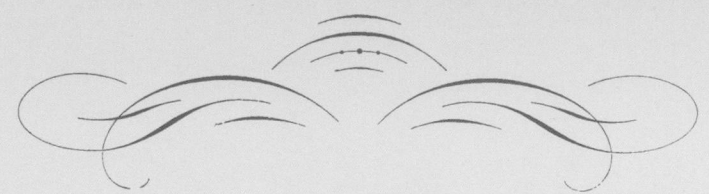

ORANGE AND GARLIC-CRUSTED LEG OF LAMB

Leg of lamb is so lean that it works beautifully with this spectacular cooking method. Basically, you encase the meat in a thick layer of oranges, rosemary and thyme, so that the lamb gets the benefits of both roasting and steaming but doesn't dry out. The resulting meat has a wonderfully fragrant, herby taste, and although the colour of the oranges fades a little during cooking, the dish still looks spectacular when it arrives at the table. I've also made this dish a fair few times with a lemon crust, which works well, as do satsumas (especially good around Christmas). Spanish blood oranges are particularly good to use when they are in season because of their intense flavour and colour. Avoid navel oranges, though, as they have too much pith.

SERVES 8

1 leg of lamb

FOR THE CRUST
4 oranges, chopped into chunks
8 fat garlic cloves, peeled and roughly chopped
3 tablespoons fresh rosemary leaves
2 tablespoons fresh thyme leaves
1 teaspoon salt

FOR GRAVY
250ml white wine
250ml chicken stock
juice of ¼ orange
green beans and roast potatoes, to serve

Remove the leg of lamb from the fridge and set aside to return to room temperature. Preheat the oven to 200°C. Combine all the crust ingredients in a food-processor and whizz until the mixture has the texture of hummus. Spread a small pool of the paste on the base of a large roasting tin and place the lamb on top of it. Now spread the rest of the paste all over the lamb until it's completely covered. Cover loosely with foil and roast for 1½ hours (or longer if you like your lamb well done).

Now for the gravy: pour the wine and stock into a saucepan and simmer it for 10 minutes, then add the orange juice. Finally, turn the heat off and cover with a lid to keep warm.

When the lamb is cooked, remove it from the roasting tin, place on a board and cover with foil to rest for 30 minutes. Scrape most of the crust out of the roasting tin, reserving a good couple of handfuls to use for the gravy. (Avoid using any burnt or blackened bits, though, as these will make the gravy taste bitter.) Add the wine, chicken stock and orange gravy to the tin and place over a low heat. Stir the reserved crust mixture into the stock a spoonful at a time, tasting each time you add, until you have a good fragrant gravy. Strain before serving.

After the lamb has rested for at least 30 minutes, carve it at the table and serve with gravy, beans and roast potatoes.

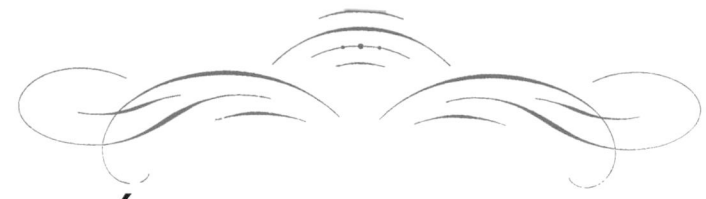

FLAMBÉED LAMB CHOPS

OK, let's all just calm down before this gets out of hand. I know that a lot of blokes (myself included) like to play with fire in the kitchen, and that any food TV series needs a gratuitous shot of culinary conflagration in the title sequence so that we all know how dramatic it's all going to be, but listen: you really *could* burn the house down when you flambé. Worse, you could ruin your steak. There's a time and a place – and a cut of meat – for flames. (Don't try to flambé a rack of lamb or you'll be very sorry indeed.) This recipe is for the classic seventies version of flambéing, where the cooked dish is finished at the table with a slosh of brandy and then lit. When the flames have died down, it's time to tuck in.

Why flambé? I like to flambé cognac in the final stages of making chicken liver parfait to prevent the alcohol giving the dish a slightly cloying taste. I also like to deglaze the steak pan with a splash of dessert wine and burn it off to make my sauce – although that's largely a futile attempt to look butch for Georgia (who generally raises her eyes to the heavens and says 'well *done*, Sweetpea' as if to a toddler in a sandpit). That said, both these tasks can be carried out by calmly simmering and reducing rather than flambéing. Flambéing at the table is good when you want a slight caramel singeing to the dish and you're using the pan juices as a sauce, too.

NB: If you like your pan to burst into flames on the hob when you add some wine for flavour (which is fun, but not what this recipe is for), *please* make sure that you turn off your extractor fan over the hob, otherwise it can suck the flames into it and start melting. And let's be sensible here: if you have a low, wooden ceiling, don't flambé at all. This is a good time to mention that every kitchen should have a fire extinguisher and fire blanket on hand.

This dish works just as well with good beef steaks such as sirloin, ribeye or T-bone (although I'd leave out the rosemary). Don't use fillet steak, though – why cook it when you can make carpaccio out of it?

SERVES 4

8 thick lamb chump chops,
    loin chops or cutlets
olive oil
1 tablespoon thyme leaves
1 tablespoon rosemary leaves, chopped
3 garlic cloves, finely chopped
salt and freshly ground black pepper
2 tablespoons redcurrant jelly (or
    other good fruit jelly)
glass of white wine
2 tablespoons brandy
mashed potatoes or couscous,
    glazed carrots and peas, to serve

Lay the lamb chops on a plate or tray and pour olive oil over so they are coated. Scatter half the thyme, rosemary and garlic over them, season with salt and pepper and turn them, rubbing in the flavourings with your hands. Cover and set aside at room temperature to marinate for about 30 minutes while you prepare your side dishes (I'd recommend mashed potatoes or couscous, glazed carrots and peas).

Preheat the oven to its lowest setting for keeping the steaks warm later. Put a large frying pan over a high heat and when it's nice and hot, carefully add the steaks (they may spit so a splashguard would come in handy). Fry the chops for 3 minutes on one side, then turn and cook for a further 2 minutes. They should be lightly, crisply browned on both sides, but still springy to the touch. (Bear in mind that they will continue to cook a little while resting.) Turn off the heat then remove the steaks to a plate, cover with foil and place in the oven to keep warm.

Carefully pour off excess fat into a cup, leaving a couple of tablespoons in the pan. Add the remaining herbs and garlic, the redcurrant jelly and the wine, then simmer until the gravy has reduced by two thirds and is nice and sticky. Turn off the heat, then replace the steaks in the pan, along with any meat juices, and turn them to coat.

Place all your side dishes on the table and put the frying pan in the middle of the table on a heatproof surface (I usually just use a chopping board). Heat up (but don't boil) the brandy in another small pan (it may not ignite if cold). Pour over the brandy and ignite it straight away. Wait until the flames have died down, then tuck in.

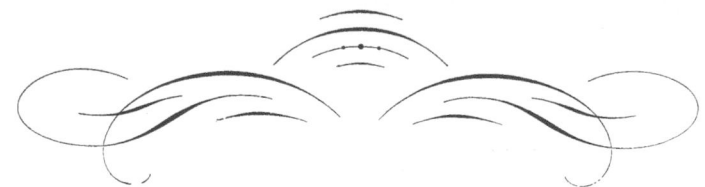

TAGINE OF LAMB WITH APRICOTS AND PRUNES

You don't need a proper tagine to make this Moroccan classic – a casserole with a good lid will do – but there is a certain spectacle to be had from placing this extraordinary clay witch's hat on the table. If you've got your own clay tagine, yes, you are supposed to put it directly on the heat on your hob, though it feels uncomfortable to do so.

I should add that although this dish needs a few hours of cooking time, it's not one of those slow-cooked dishes for which you can use cheap cuts of lamb like shanks – you really need to use leg or trimmed shoulder meat.

SERVES 6

1kg diced leg of lamb, or lamb
    shoulder, trimmed of most of the fat
4 tablespoons olive oil
1 large onion, finely chopped
4 large garlic cloves, finely chopped
2 cinnamon sticks, or 1 teaspoon
    ground cinnamon
1 teaspoon ground coriander
1 teaspoon ground cumin
400g tin of chickpeas, drained
400g tin of chopped plum tomatoes
400ml chicken stock
2cm piece of fresh root ginger, grated
250g dried apricots and/or prunes
1 strip of orange peel
500g butternut squash, peeled and
    cut into chunks
a bunch of coriander, finely chopped
    (stalks chopped and reserved)
500g couscous and harissa paste,
    to serve

Heat 2 tablespoons olive oil in a casserole or tagine then brown the lamb, a batch at a time, over a high heat. Remove the lamb and set aside.

Reduce the heat, add the onion and fry until soft and browned. Stir in the garlic, cinnamon, ground coriander and cumin and fry for 1 minute, then add the chickpeas, tomatoes, chicken stock, ginger and dried fruit. Stir, bring to a simmer, then cover and simmer very gently for 1½ hours. Add the orange peel, butternut squash and the coriander stalks. Simmer very gently for a further 30 minutes.

Meanwhile, prepare the couscous. In a heatproof bowl, pour boiling water over the couscous until it's covered (use good-quality stock, if you prefer). Cover and leave to soak for 15 minutes, then check that the couscous is tender (add a few tablespoons more boiling water if not and leave to rest for a further 5 minutes). Stir in the chopped coriander leaves and 2 tablespoons of olive oil and season to taste.

Serve the tagine with the couscous and some harissa, for your friends to add as they wish.

SUCKLING PIG

There's something undeniably decadent about serving a whole suckling pig. In many ways it feels like the ultimate feast – a whole, beautiful young piglet cooked to crisp, succulent perfection. It's a treat that should be kept for very special occasions, not least because suckling pigs are very expensive. Perhaps surprisingly, however, they are pretty easy to cook. I don't think there's much point in trying out new cooking methods and strange flavour combinations here; after all, how much more extraordinary can you get than serving a whole pig!

The one thing you absolutely must remember is to measure your oven before you order your pig – you can either fit a whole small one in a 90cm-wide oven or, depending on the number of friends you're planning to feed, have a larger one cut in half, to cook in two pieces that you can put back together for serving.

Not all suckling pigs are equal – the one in the picture fed about 30 hungry people, but I've had a smaller one, just big enough to feed 10. They usually weigh anything from 5 to 15kg and you can even get really mini ones that will serve 4–6 people, but they make for an extremely expensive meal, and in any case their tiny size can be a little disconcerting even for the most committed carnivore. Any good butcher should be able to get a decent-sized one for you, although you may need to order it a week in advance. There are also specialist online and mail order sources (see Suppliers, page 218). You will need to allow about 500g of whole pig weight per person.

You can cook a suckling pig in an oven very easily, but for more dramatic effect, cook it on a spit barbecue (mine is a brilliant Turkish affair with a basic but very effective little motor, built for lamb work), which adds to the feast atmosphere.

THE WHOLE HOG
If you fancy cooking a whole full-sized pig, and have 100 great mates you'd like to share it with (at a wedding, perhaps), there are two ways of going about it:

1. THE COMPLEX AND EXPENSIVE APPROACH
This involves building your own spit mechanism. A good size pig for a hog roast weighs around 30–50kg (it becomes impractical to roast a hog larger than this), and you'll need some serious kit to cope with spinning a piece of meat this size. If you have lots of storage space, a welding kit and the expertise to create some solid ironmongery (or the cash to pay someone else to do it for you) then go ahead and build a sturdy adjustable steel spit and buy a motor and the bits to go with it. I have two friends who have this kit (both are farmers, with barns and oxyacetylene torches and their own pigs to roast), and the parties they throw are fantastic. Hugh Fearnley-Whittingstall's *Meat* has some pretty detailed instructions for going about your own hog roast.

2. GETTING THE PROFESSIONALS IN
There is a second, albeit less romantic, way to stage a hog roast feast, which is to hire professionals to do it for you! Look, I know it would be lovely to do it all yourself, but you're probably only going to roast a whole hog a few times in your life, and there are lots of companies who rent out their kit, often with the ready-to-cook pig delivered with the spit roast. It'll cost you several hundred pounds, but for that you'll be feeding a hundred or so people, and these companies will deliver the kit, take it away, and even leave someone on hand to roast the hog for you if you so wish. The kit is often fired by gas rather than wood or charcoal, but it's still spectacular and huge, yet practical. (See Suppliers, page 218, for some companies who supply all the kit.)

10kg suckling pig, cut in half if
    necessary to fit into your oven
    (discuss this with your supplier)
a large handful fresh thyme
a large handful fresh rosemary,
    on the stalks
8 bay leaves
10 garlic cloves, peeled
salt and freshly ground black pepper
1 apple
olive oil
apple sauce, roast potatoes, peas and
    carrots, to serve

Let your pig come up to room temperature before cooking
– this could take 1–2 hours, depending on its size. Preheat
the oven to 190°C. Wash the pig inside and out and pat dry
with kitchen paper. Place one of the grill-shelves from your
oven on your kitchen surface, lay plenty of foil on it, and
place the pig on top. Rub salt all over the skin, inside and
out, and then put the herbs and garlic inside the stomach
cavity to flavour the pig while it's roasting. Put a stone
between its teeth to keep the mouth open while roasting
(you'll replace it later with the apple), then rub all over
with olive oil. Wrap the pig loosely in the foil.

Roast in the oven for 3 hours (approx 20–25 minutes per
500g for smaller pigs up to 6kg), basting every 30 minutes
(and swapping the top and bottom trays if the pig is in two
halves). Remove the foil from the top of the pig and turn
the heat up to 220°C and continue to roast for a further
20 minutes to crisp the skin. Check that the pig is cooked
by sticking a long skewer into it at the thickest point (the
juices should run clear or yellow).

Bring the pig to the table (don't you dare carve it without
showing everyone!) and, if practical, place it in the middle
of the table and allow everyone to carve their own pork.
Serve with apple sauce, roast potatoes, peas and carrots.

7

DESSERTS

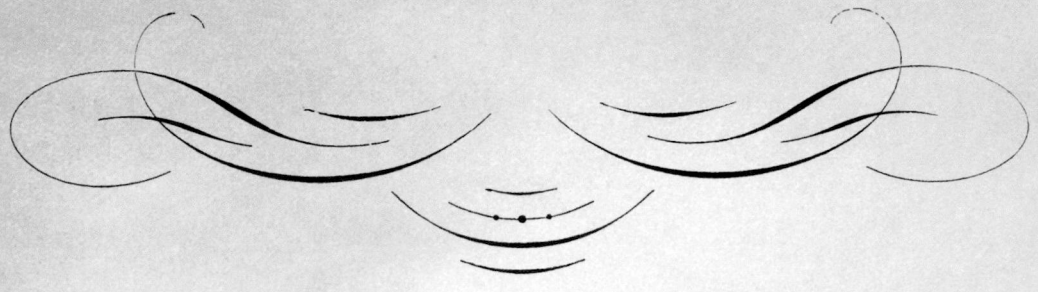

THE RECIPES HERE ARE MOSTLY SIMPLE and easily achievable to the extent of laziness. For instance, there's really nothing more to Bowls of Sweets than some sweets and a bowl to put them in. I couldn't resist giving you a recipe for liquid nitrogen-made ice cream – even though I'm aware that you may not have access to the stuff – but for the most part these are intriguing but dead simple desserts, which is the way I think desserts should be. My friends are always over the moon to get anything at the end of a meal (or are too full to contemplate another mouthful), so they are invariably happy with whatever I rustle up. Our family favourite is Space Dust-encrusted Pineapple Carpaccio, which is much easier than it sounds to make, yet it's a riotous combination of flavour and physical sensations.

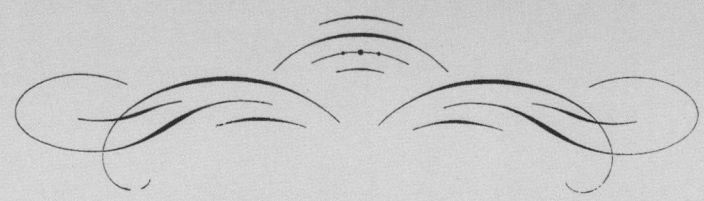

CHOCOLATE FRUITFEST

There's nothing more to these than fruit dipped into melted chocolate, yet when I serve them to my friends they always go a little bit crazy. These are also a very sneaky way to get picky kids to eat fresh fruit (and if you use good dark chocolate, you can even claim that they're healthy). Don't worry if you don't have any greaseproof paper – you can make these on any non-stick surface such as a baking sheet or frying pan.

SERVES 6

750g assorted fruit: grapes,
    strawberries, cherries, blueberries,
    blackcurrants or fig slices
100g good-quality dark chocolate,
    broken into chunks

Wash and prepare your fruit: pull the grapes off the stem but leave cherry and strawberry stalks on, then lay on some kitchen paper to dry and put in the fridge to chill.

Melt the chocolate in a heatproof bowl over a saucepan of barely simmering water. Stir it just until it melts (you don't want to heat it any more than necessary), then remove from the heat.

Lay some greaseproof paper on a tray (or a non-stick roasting tin) that will fit in your fridge. Dip the chilled fruit into the melted chocolate and lay on the paper. Store in the fridge until you're ready to serve.

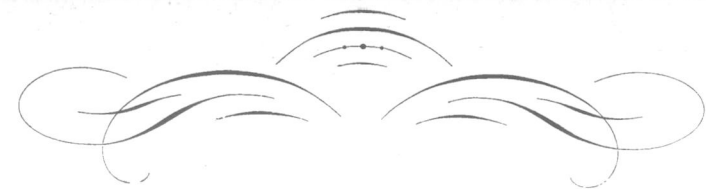

FLUORESCENT JELLIES

This isn't a cheat, and it's not an optical illusion, these are simply gin and tonic jellies made by adding gelatin to G&T and leaving them to set. So why are they glowing that fantastic ghostly colour? The answer is that quinine (the bitter flavouring in tonic water) glows under UV fluorescent light. If you want to serve this to kids or teetotallers, it works just as well without the gin.

The great thing about G&T jelly (other than its glowiness) is that you can serve it either before the meal as a solid G&T, complete with its bubbles captured in the jelly (yes, the picture below really does show a G&T with trapped bubbles, and the jelly even retains a little fizz), or you can have them after your meal as a wonderfully crazy dessert. Either way, it's best to place them all on the table without drawing attention to them, and then switch on your fluorescent bulb and place it as close to the jellies as is safe before you switch off the lights.

Just buy a UV fluorescent light (easily found at hardware stores or on the web) and you're away. The bigger the bulb, the better the glow. I should add that the inspiration for these jellies comes from my bonkers chemist friend Dr Andrea Sella and the equally bonkers Bompass & Parr, jellymongers to the great and the good, who kindly showed me and some fascinated kids how to make a fluorescent St Paul's Cathedral for my *Gastronuts* TV show.

MAKES 2 LITRES (ENOUGH FOR 8 HIGHBALL GLASSES OR 3–4 JELLY MOULDS)

2 packs of leaf gelatin (enough to firmly set 2 litres – usually about 50 per cent more than listed on the packet)
500ml good-quality gin (you can substitute this for extra tonic if you don't want to serve alcohol)
juice of 3 large lemons
1.5 litres tonic water (chilled before use if possible)
8 lemon slices, to garnish (optional)

Cut the gelatin leaves into small pieces using scissors and put them into a large heatproof bowl. Pour 250ml of gin over the gelatin and leave for 10 minutes to start it softening. Put the bowl in a microwave and heat on full power for 1½ minutes (or place the bowl over a saucepan of boiling water), then stir until the gelatin has completely dissolved. Don't let it boil.

Stir the remaining gin and the lemon juice into the gelatin, then add the chilled tonic water, pouring it in as carefully as you can to avoid it fizzing (you want to lock in all those bubbles).

If you are using jelly moulds, lightly grease them inside using vegetable oil on a piece of kitchen paper. Pour the G&T mixture, equally carefully, into your jelly moulds or glasses, garnish with lemon slices, if using, and place in the fridge to set for about 6 hours.

Serve under UV light. The darker it is, the better the effect, so serve at night, with the lights turned out and the UV bulb as close to the jellies as possible!

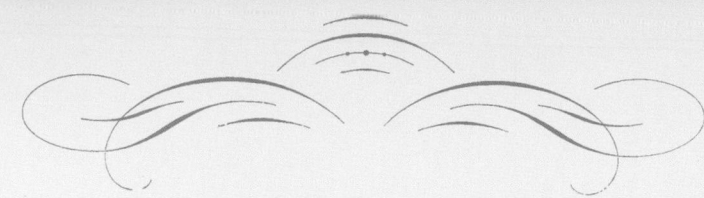

LIQUID NITROGEN AND LEMONGRASS ICE CREAM

Liquid nitrogen boils at −196°C, which really is very cold indeed. On one hand, this makes it great fun to play with, as you can pour it directly into a substance that you want to chill, releasing plumes of mist, delighting the kids and scaring the cat. On the other hand, its instability – and the danger that it will freeze your hand so cold that it will snap off – means that liquid nitrogen can be hard to find down at the corner shop. Fortunately for me, my great chemist friend, Dr Sella, has a good supply of the stuff, and, for a contribution to the college Petri-dish fund, he will let me have some.

One very strange fact about liquid nitrogen is that it's an incredibly cheap substance. The downside is that you need some very expensive high-tech storage facilities to keep it at home, and special double-walled flasks called Dewar flasks to transport it in. Liquid nitrogen is distilled from liquid air (air that has been compressed and cooled to temperatures so low that it condenses to a liquid), and seeing as our atmosphere is 78 per cent nitrogen (and 21 per cent oxygen), there's a lot of it around. It's perfectly safe to pour liquid nitrogen into your food as long as it's not too cold to bear – it all boils away as soon as it warms above -196°C and in any case we breath the stuff all the time. It's even used in some food-production processes, for instance mayonnaise-making, to cool food quickly so that bacteria are less likely to multiply in it. Weird, huh?

Dr Sella loves playing with this stuff (he dips his finger in it, which is apparently fine as long as you take it straight out), and I've even seen him pouring it in his mouth and spitting it out to make instant snow. If you ever manage to get your hands on some liquid nitrogen, *do not try this at home* – Andrea can do this because he is a chemist and entirely bonkers.

This recipe is actually a very delicious and practical one that you can make with or without liquid nitrogen – for instance with an ice-cream maker. The original version had jellyfish in, but what with one thing and another, that seemed like overkill.

SERVES 6

3 lemongrass stalks, outer skin peeled
    off, insides finely chopped
175ml double cream
175ml coconut milk
150ml whole milk
4 eggs, yolks only
100g caster sugar
zest of 1 lime
liquid nitrogen

Put the first four ingredients in a saucepan. Bring to the boil over a medium heat, then remove the pan from the heat and leave to cool for 5 minutes. Meanwhile, in a separate bowl, beat the egg yolks, sugar and lime zest until pale. Place the pan of lemongrass mixture over a low heat, and add the egg and sugar mixture. Heat gently, stirring all the time, until the mixture thickens slightly to form a light custard. Don't let it boil or overheat, otherwise the eggs will curdle. Strain out the lemongrass.

If you have an ice-cream maker, use it to make the ice cream. Otherwise, put your safety goggles on and carefully stir in the liquid nitrogen a splash at a time, letting each splash boil off before you add the next one, until the ice cream freezes. Warning: if you pour in too much nitrogen at a time, you are likely to create super-chilled lumps rather than a nice, smooth, edible mixture. Don't turn the ice cream solid or it will be too cold to eat.

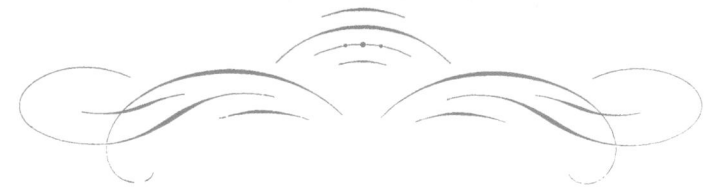

LIMONCELLO FRUIT JELLYFEST

These are ridiculously easy to make. You *could* create your own homemade flavours from gelatin-based concoctions, but if you're going to do that, I'd save the effort for making the fluorescent G&T jellies on page 194, or for flights of elderflower-based fancy when the season is right (when spring is about to tumble into summer). No, for these, I'd use just good-quality concentrated lemon jelly, adding a sour kick of lemon juice to balance the sweetness and a fat slug of limoncello (a delicious lemon liqueur). If you don't have any limoncello, vodka is a pretty good substitute. (For committed jellyboozers, here's a fascinating article on how much alcohol you can add to jelly before it refuses to set: http://www.myscienceproject.org/j-shot.html). If you're serving the jellies to kids, you should obviously leave out the booze.

SERVES 6

1 packet of good-quality concentrated
   lemon jelly
juice of ½ lemon
150ml limoncello or vodka
assorted fruit (but not figs or pineapple,
   which stop the jelly from setting)

Make up the jelly according to the instructions on the packet, but use only half the quantity of water called for, to allow for the lemon juice and spirits. Add the lemon juice and limoncello or vodka and stir in. Divide the fruit between small glasses and pour over the jelly mixture. Place the jellies in the fridge and leave to set for at least 4 hours.

CHOCOLATE-COVERED CRUNCHY HONEYCOMB

I recently spent six days experimenting with honeycomb, malt and chocolate combinations to try to recreate Maltesers. Never before has so much effort and pain been expended for eight minutes of culinary telly fluff. I don't mind telling you that I nearly went mad trying to get the balance right (though my rabid children reaped the benefits: 'hmm, not quite crispy enough, Daddy, try again').

The difficulty in Malteser-making lies not in the honeycomb-making. No, the trouble crops up when you add malt to the mixture, which messes with the delicate chemistry of sugar-setting, and as for trying to scoop perfect balls out of the mixture…. Suffice to say, there's a good reason why the sweets companies have multimillion-pound factories and teams of people who dedicate their lives to creating the perfect chocolatey snack. (If you're interested, they make perfect malty honeycomb balls by cooking them in a partial vacuum so that the bubbles develop just right, then coat them several times and spin them on rollers so that they set perfectly.) I'd just like to add that on the day of filming, my slightly gnarly-looking versions won 75 per cent of the vote in a blind taste-test. I suspect the audience was being kind to me – they could tell by the feel of my knobbly versions which was which!

You can make all manner of fun shapes with the honeycomb, and you can also cover them in chocolate to make your own version of Crunchie bars.

butter, for greasing
350g sugar
100ml honey
2 tablespoons glucose syrup
1 ½ teaspoons bicarbonate of soda
500g good-quality chocolate (dark or
    milk), broken into small chunks

Grease two large baking sheets or roasting tins with butter. Put the sugar, honey, glucose syrup and 100ml water in a large saucepan and heat gently, stirring frequently with a long wooden spoon until the sugar has entirely dissolved. Now turn the heat up to medium and let it boil. The mixture needs to reach the 'hard crack' stage, which is around 155°C (if you have a jam thermometer), or when it turns a dark caramel colour. This should take about 30 minutes.

Turn off the heat and quickly stir in the bicarbonate of soda. The mixture will slowly start to foam up, and as it does so, pour half of it onto one baking sheet or roasting tin. On the other, try to make a series of dollops in fun shapes. (If it's too tricky, just make another big blob!). Leave the honeycomb to set for 2–3 hours – it needs to dry out thoroughly.

Break up the large blocks of solid honeycomb into chunks (a hammer or rolling pin may be handy here). You could stop right here and eat it as it is, but if you fancy going one step further you can cover it with chocolate to great effect.

Melt the chocolate in a heatproof bowl over a saucepan of barely simmering water. Stir the chocolate just until it melts (you don't want to heat it any more than necessary), then remove from the heat.

Lay some greaseproof paper on a tray (or a non-stick roasting tin) that will fit in your fridge. Dip each chunk of honeycomb into the chocolate and lay it on the greaseproof paper. Put in the fridge to set.

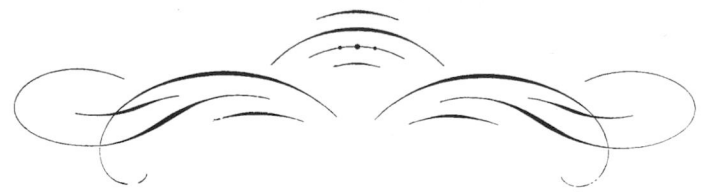

AFFOGATO

Never has so much culinary wonder come from so little effort. Affogato is a Milanese speciality that involves pouring a strong little espresso over a ball of vanilla ice cream. And that's it. You do, of course, need the means to make an espresso, but beyond that, there's nothing to it.

SERVES 4

500g good vanilla ice cream
4 shots good, hot espresso

Place four glasses in the freezer to chill them a little (skip this bit if you're too hungry to wait), and when they're frosty, put a scoop of vanilla ice cream in each of them. Pour a shot of espresso over the top of each one and serve, with some amaretti biscuits, if available (see page 206).

BOWLS OF SWEETS

It's got to be the laziest dessert on the planet, but when you fill a few bowls with chocolates and sweets and plonk them on the table after a big meal, everyone's eyes light up with childish pleasure. We all love a sophisticated fine pastry or refined fondant or coulis every now and then, but there's an extraordinarily joyous release when you indulge simpler pleasures. You'll wonder why you don't do it more often.

The only advice I can give is that the more childish or nostalgic the sweets, the more your friends will love them. My friends particularly love jelly babies, Smarties, Sherbert Fountains and Maltesers. (And the latter are particularly good when melted into a coffee!)

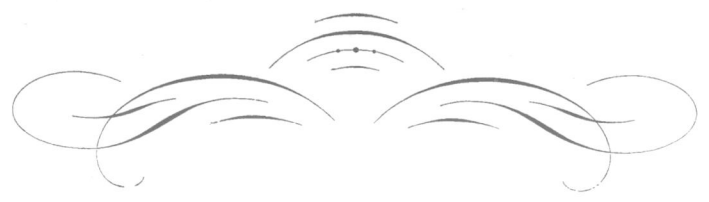

AMARETTI FUN

Amaretti are light almond biscuits that are very nice to eat at the end of a meal with your coffee. But it's not so much their flavour that excites me as their packaging and the fun you can have with it. They usually arrive in pretty tins or boxes, but crucially, each biscuit also comes wrapped in an extraordinary tissue paper that is extremely light and yet has enough structure to enable it to stand up on its own if rolled. This means that if you flatten out a wrapper then roll it up, you can set light to it so that it burns down to the bottom and then flies up into the air.

When I first started doing this many years ago, the paper could be held in your hand and lit. If you were brave enough, it would lift up just before it scorched your hand. But the manufacturers seem to have changed their packaging material, and there's now no way you can do this without rolling up the wrapper and carefully laying it on a plate before lighting it.

Here's what you do. First locate your fire extinguisher in case it all goes horribly wrong, then unwrap your amaretti and flatten the piece of paper out on the table. Next, roll it, stand it up on its end on a plate and set light to the top of it with a match. Sit back and keep a wary eye on it: the paper should burn down to the bottom and then, just when you're beginning to think it hasn't worked, it should lift up into the air – often a metre or so. Keep an eye out in case the embers don't go out and the burning wrapper sets light to something.

WARNING: only do this if you have a fire extinguisher to hand and, of course, please don't encourage your kids to play with fire!

8

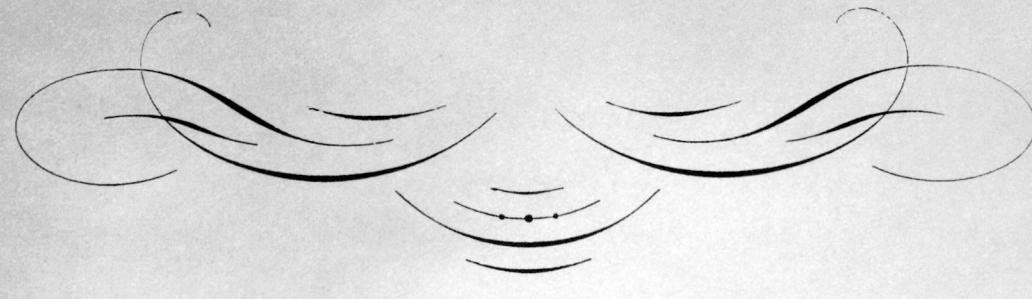

DRINKS

EXTRAORDINARY DRINKS are the icing on the cake of any extraordinary feast. You don't have to make them, but some of these are so simple, it seems rude not to, especially the fresh herb teas which are an easy, yet sensuous and intriguing way to end a feast. And if you want to turn your dinner into a wild party, I offer you this one word of advice: cocktails. In my experience, any evening that starts with margarita invariably ends in riot. One cocktail sprinkles a little magic over dinner, and five cocktails generally means that you could serve baked beans on toast and still have a wild time. Just don't drink so many that you don't remember the meal the following day. That way madness lies, and anyway the whole point is to make a meal that everyone remembers forever. Bon chance, mon brave.

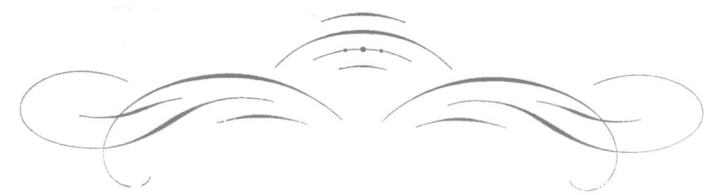

FRESH HERBAL TEAS

Fresh herbs are perfect for instant herbal tea so it seems silly not to use them. I've always got a bunch of thyme knocking around in the fridge, as well as a thumb of ginger, and there'll usually be a bunch of rosemary, mint or coriander there too. Those posh herbal tea bags never get used quickly enough, leaving me with a cupboard full of out-of-date boxes. In my experience there are very few people who drink herbal teas all the time, but lots of my friends do like to sip something light and herby late in the night after I've spent an evening stuffing them full of extraordinary food. I've now stopped buying posh teas and I just use what's good and fresh.

My favourite way to serve herbal teas is to put mugs of hot water on the table alongside a few bundles of herbs, some slices of ginger and lemon and some sugar, and let everyone make their own fragrant combinations. Fresh thyme is a winner, and rosemary is delicious too, despite the fact that it has a reputation for bitterness when fresh. Bay leaf is good, parsley is wonderfully delicate, cinnamon and star anise are very interesting, and lightly spicy.

You have to drink the tea with the herbs still in it, but as long as they're on a sprig rather than in lots of little bits, I prefer this to a soggy tea bag floating around. You can also buy empty tea bags ready for filling with your own herbs and spices (see Suppliers, page 218). So instead of buying lots of expensive boxes of obscure flavour combinations, just open up your herb and spice cupboard and go to town.

MY SUGGESTIONS
- rosemary
- basil
- thyme
- mint
- ginger and lemon
- dill
- fresh rose petals
- lemongrass
- bay leaves
- coriander
- parsley
- cinnamon
- a whole lime (the oils in the zest ooze out!)
- galangal

Serve mugs of piping hot water with a selection of herbs and spices for your friends to help themselves, and put honey and sugar on the table, too.

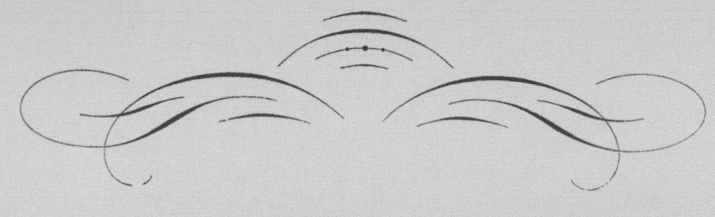

SLOE GIN

Sloes, also known as blackthorns, are little wild plums the size and colour of a deep-red/purple grape. They are very astringent, so aren't much good for eating, but they make an extraordinary deep-red and full-flavoured drink when steeped in gin for a few months. I've never seen sloes on sale in shops, but if you find them while out foraging, grab them to make some of this. You'll also need a wide-necked bottle or a resealable jar, washed out with boiling water.

37.5ml (half a bottle) gin
60g caster sugar
½ teaspoon almond essence
250g sloes, washed and patted dry

Pour the gin, sugar and almond essence into a sterilised bottle or jar and swill it around until the sugar has mostly dissolved. Prick the washed sloes all over with a needle – at least five pricks per sloe – then add them to the liquid and seal the bottle or jar tightly. Add a label and write the date on it. The sloes need to steep in the gin for at least 3 months. (Write the 'ready' date on too, to remind you.)

Store the bottle in a dark place and shake it every now and then – once a week if you can remember. You can strain the sloe gin (through a piece of muslin or a clean tea-towel) and rebottle it any time between 3 and 12 months after initial bottling. Serve as a neat liqueur.

LEMONADE

This lemonade tastes like you've squeezed pure sunshine into a glass and just added bubbles.

MAKES 2 LITRES

250g sugar
6 lemons

TO SERVE
1.25 litres still or sparkling water
lots of ice

Put 200ml water and the sugar in a pan and warm over a low heat, stirring until the sugar has dissolved. Peel or grate the zest of one of the lemons, then juice all six lemons and stir zest and juice into the syrup. Pour into a bottle or jug and place in the fridge until fully chilled (about 30–60 minutes). To serve, mix with sparkling water and add ice.

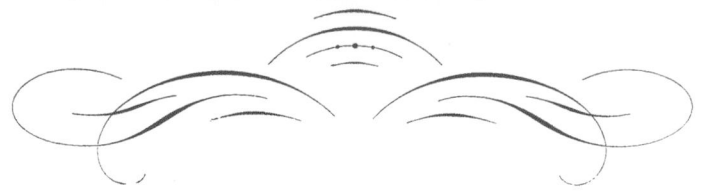

GINGER BEER

My mum always had a few bottles of ginger beer brewing, and every now and then one would blow up, with an impressive KaBOOOM. If you want to avoid explosions, it's simple: use plastic fizzy drink bottles, which are made to cope with tremendous pressure.

This recipe takes only 20 minutes or so to make, but the ginger beer needs to be left to brew for a day or three before it's ready to drink. You'll need 5 litres worth of bottles and a large saucepan that will hold 5 litres of beer.

MAKES ABOUT 5 LITRES

500g caster sugar
2 lemons, thickly sliced
2 tablespoons finely chopped fresh ginger
1 teaspoon cream of tartar
1½ teaspoons dried fast-action yeast
  (bread-maker yeast is fine)

Measure 1.5 litres of water into a large saucepan and add the sugar, lemon slices, ginger and cream of tartar. Bring to the boil, stirring the liquid to dissolve the sugar. Simmer for 5 minutes, then remove from the heat and add a further 3 litres of cold water. Sprinkle in the yeast, stir it through and put a lid on the pan. Remove the pan to a cool place and leave it overnight.

In the morning, wash the bottles in very hot water. Strain the beer through a sieve to catch the ginger, then pour it into the bottles, leaving 5cm of air at the top of each one. Screw the lids firmly onto the bottles and put them in a cool place to brew. It's this fermentation process that makes the beer fizzy and it will take 12–48 hours, depending on the temperature, for it to develop the right amount of fizz.

AN INSTANT VARIATION
If you feel you can't wait 2 days, try making this instant version. Mix together 1 thumb-sized piece of fresh ginger, peeled and grated, 75g unrefined sugar and the zest and juice of 2 lemons. Leave to rest for 30 minutes, then sieve and mix with fizzy water to taste. It's nice, but it's a different beast to the fermented version.

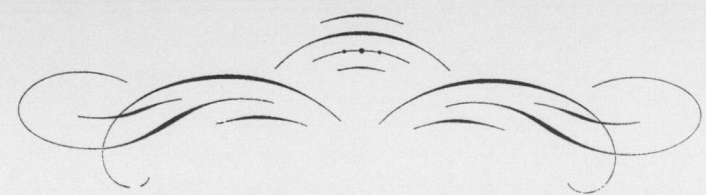

GATES-PEMBERTON
MEGABRAND-SLAYING COLA

It's the ultimate secret recipe, jealously guarded by the world's largest drinks company, so there's a lovely little frisson of excitement when you create your own cola: will you bust the mega-brand? When you serve it to your friends, will the doors burst open and a SWAT team storm your kitchen and whisk you and your refreshing beverage off to an undisclosed location for interrogation? It would be a great story to tell – if they let you go before pudding.

Coca-Cola began life in 1885 when the first version was invented as a medicine by a chap called John Pemberton. It was initially an alcoholic drink called Pemberton's French Wine Cola, but was changed to non-alcoholic Coca-Cola a year later. It was, by all accounts, quite a zippy little brew at first, made as it was from highly stimulating coca (from which cocaine is derived), caffeine-rich kola nuts and an ingredient called damiana, which is purported to be both an aphrodisiac and, perhaps more plausibly, a cannabis-like psychoactive drug.

I recently re-created Coke on a TV show, which meant I was given the time of a lovely researcher called Natalie and a decent budget to buy lots of specialist ingredients to experiment with. I tried to perfect two recipes: a natural version using ingredients that are easy to find at your local shops, and a second one based on Pemberton's original recipe (or, at least, a recipe I found that claimed to be his original). My local pharmacy nearly called the cops when I asked if they could get their hands on any food-grade cocaine, and they nearly refused to serve me the Pro-Plus tablets (for the caffeine).

I tried all the different concoctions out on my girls, who both went a little bonkers after tasting the kola nuts (they'd never even drunk Coke, bless 'em), but as taste-testers they were rubbish: they just preferred whichever drink had the most sugar in. I did a lot of tinkering, but finally I got pretty close to the original. Then I decided to go one step further and make some adjustments to the basic recipe to create something I thought tasted *better* than the original. When I hit on something that I really loved (a little more floral, slightly more sour, slightly less bitter but slightly less sweet than modern Coke), I took all my syrups along to the TV studio. We had a blind taste test with the TV show audience, and I am proud to say that I won by a landslide, with 85 per cent claiming to prefer my brew.

The flavour base of cola is a combination of citrus fruit oils (from the zest), a few of the sweeter tasting spices, sourness from citrus fruit, and a bucketload of sweetness from refined and unrefined sugars. If you can lay your hands on some kola nuts, they give a great bitterness – and whizziness as they are rich in caffeine! If you use the food-grade essential oils, you'll need to measure them using a set of micro-scales or a syringe bought from your local chemist.

Right then, all I need for world domination is a multimillion-pound marketing campaign, an integrated global distribution network, a bit of seed funding and a bigger pan.

MAKES ENOUGH SYRUP FOR ABOUT 6 LITRES OF COLA

FOR THE SYRUP
750g sugar
10 caffeine pills (optional), ground to
    powder in pestle and mortar (this
    will give about half the amount of
    caffeine found in a regular cola)
100ml freshly squeezed lime juice
10g citric acid
1.5ml vanilla extract
2 tablespoons caramel
25g kola nuts, finely crushed (optional)
grated zest of 2 lemons

FOR THE FLAVOURING
1ml food-grade orange oil
0.5ml food-grade cinnamon oil
0.5ml food-grade nutmeg oil
0.5ml food-grade neroli oil
0.25ml food-grade coriander oil

TO SERVE
soda water

Pour 500ml water into a pan and bring to the boil. Turn off
the heat, then add the sugar and stir until dissolved. Stir in
all the remaining syrup ingredients and set aside.

Put all the flavoured oils in a small blender (it has to be
small, otherwise the blades won't reach the level of the
oils). Add 2 tablespoons of the syrup, or enough to cover
the blades of the blender. Blend until the liquids have
emulsified, then pour the contents of the blender into the
remaining syrup (washing the blender out with a little extra
syrup to get every last drop) and set aside to cool for 1 hour.

Strain the mixture through a piece of muslin or a clean
tea-towel into a jug, then transfer to a bottle. To serve, add
240ml soda water to 60ml of syrup; taste to see if it's to
your satisfaction, adjusting the concentration if needed.

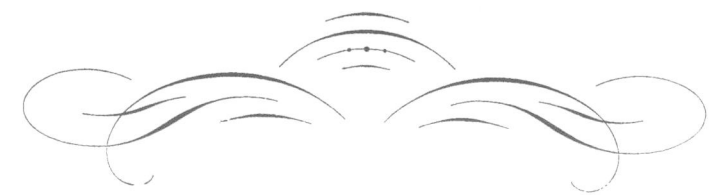

FOUR CLASSIC COCKTAILS

There really is nothing better to kick off a big night in than a walloping good cocktail, especially if it's a Martini. These outrageous concoctions are a beguiling mix of danger and sophistication resolved into a gasping shock of sheer alcoholic power. Be careful, though: the great MFK Fisher – an extraordinary woman who vies with Brillat-Savarin as my favourite, funniest deadest food writer – once wrote that 'One Martini is just right. Two Martinis are too many. Three Martinis are never enough'. I've experimented with lots of different cocktails, but the reality is that I've never really needed any more than these four classics.

MARTINI

For sophistication and sheer power – careful, now. This is the classic very dry version.

SERVES 1

2 shots (50ml) fine gin
¼ shot (6–7ml) dry vermouth
    (i.e. Martini)
a handful of ice
a green olive or a long, thin strip of
    lemon peel, to serve

Pour the gin and vermouth into a cocktail shaker, add the ice and shake to mix. Pour into a Martini glass, add either an olive or a strip of lemon peel to garnish and serve.

DANNY'S MARGARITA

If you're after a wild, whooping party atmosphere.

SERVES 1

2 shots (50ml) tequila
1 shot (25ml) Cointreau
1 shot (25ml) freshly squeezed lime juice
fine salt or popping candy (such as
    Space Dust or Pop Rocks) and a
    wedge of lime, to serve

Pour the tequila, Cointreau and lime juice into a cocktail shaker and shake well to mix. Pour the salt or popping candy onto a small plate, wipe the rim of a Martini glass with the lime slice to wet it a little, then dip it upside down on the plate to coat the rim (not too much – you don't want a mouthful of salt). Pour the cocktail into the glass and serve with the wedge of lime to suck on.

MOJITO

Dangerously easy-drinking, fun and sweet. An ad man would probably say that this is 'young-skewing'.

SERVES 1

2 teaspoons sugar
½ fresh lime, chopped into 4 pieces
10 fresh mint leaves
crushed ice (wrap ice cubes in a tea
    towel and beat with a rolling pin)
2 shots (50ml) rum
soda water, to taste

Put the sugar and lime chunks into a solid highball glass and muddle it (i.e. smush it up) with a pestle or soup spoon. Add the mint and muddle it some more. Fill the glass with crushed ice, then pour over the rum and give it a good stir. Top up the glass with soda water, stir again and serve.

COSMOPOLITAN

This can be made very conveniently in a large jug and poured out by the glass.

SERVES 1

1 shot (25ml) vodka (preferably lemon
    flavoured, but any will do)
1 shot (25ml) Cointreau or
    Grand Marnier
juice of ½ lime
2 shots (50ml) cranberry juice
ice, to serve

Pour all the ingredients except the ice into a cocktail shaker and shake to mix. Pour into a Martini glass, add ice and serve.

SUPPLIERS

Before you turn to the internet for your extraordinary supplies, take a look around your local shops: you may be surprised at how many of the ingredients mentioned in this book are available (or can easily be ordered) from specialist and ethnic sources right on your doorstep, and I'd encourage you to buy them where a friendly face can give you advice or help you source what you need. My local friendly faces are at Newington Green Fruit and Veg.

FROGS' LEGS
Available online from The Fish Society: www.thefishsociety.co.uk

RUSSIAN ROULETTE PADRÓN PEPPERS
Usually available fresh from good supermarkets, especially during the summer months (although I've also found them in early spring).
Also available mail order from Delicioso: www.delicioso.co.uk

SEED SUPPLIERS
The English Chilli Co:
www.theenglishchillicompany.co.uk
Marshalls Seeds:
www.marshalls-seeds.co.uk

WEIRD AND WONDERFUL SNACKS
Wai Yee Hong: www.waiyeehong.com
Wing Yip: www.wingyipstore.co.uk

INSECTS
Edible Unique: www.edibleunique.com
Thailand Unique:
www.thailandunique.com
Edible: www.edible.com

FOR THE LOVE OF JAMÓN
Whole Spanish hams and ham stands:

IberGour: www.ibergour.com
They sell a huge selection of whole high-end hams direct from Spain, as well as the much cheaper shoulders from the grand producers – and at the time of printing, they give away a free ham stand and knife with each ham.
Try also: www.ibericofoods.com

OSTRICH SCOTCH EGG
Available seasonally from spring to autumn from Oslinc: www.oslinc.co.uk
And from upmarket supermarkets, usually in spring.

SUCKLING PIG
Try your local butcher first (they should be able to order one for you at a decent price), but if they can't get a good suckling pig, you can buy them online from Dunstan Game:
www.dunstangame.co.uk
Forman & Field can also supply a pricey but excellent quality Pugh's piglet: www.formanandfield.com

…also Hog Roasts: hog roasting companies tend to be regional as they deliver the kit and pig and then pick it up again. Try typing 'hog roast' and your area into a search engine.

APPLE CAVIAR
Sodium alginate, calcium chloride, micro-scales and syringes are all available from MSK Ingredients:
www.msk-ingredients.com. They are very helpful, so do call if you have any queries: 01246 412211

WHOLE BAKED VACHERIN CHEESE
Vacherin Mont d'Or is available in many cheese shops and good supermarkets during the main season from autumn to spring.

It's also available online during this season from The Fine Cheese Co:
www.finecheese.co.uk

SHABU-SHABU, SUSHI & SASHIMI
Most of the major supermarkets stock the main Japanese ingredients (in their larger stores) such as sushi rice, nori seaweed, rice vinegar, soy and shoyu sauces. Ponzu (a lemony soy sauce), sesame dipping sauce and rolling mats are available from The Japan Centre:
www.japancentre.com
Japanese Kitchen:
www.japanesekitchen.co.uk

CHOCOLATE-TIN SMOKED SALMON
Hardwood or fruitwood chips are often available from the big supermarkets around summer (i.e. barbecuing) time, but are also available from many angling shops and online from For Food Smokers:
www.forfoodsmokers.co.uk

GOLDEN CHICKEN
Edible gold and silver transfer leaf (buy 23ct or over):
Tiranti: www.tiranti.co.uk
Gold Leaf Supplies:
www.goldleafsupplies.co.uk

FLUORESCENT JELLIES
UV lamps can be bought from Lyco: www.lyco.co.uk

SPACE DUST-ENCRUSTED PINEAPPLE CARPACCIO
Cybercandy: www.cybercandy.co.uk
Handy Candy: www.handycandy.co.uk

FRESH HERB TEAS
Empty, fillable tea bags can be bought from Teeportal: www.teeportal.de

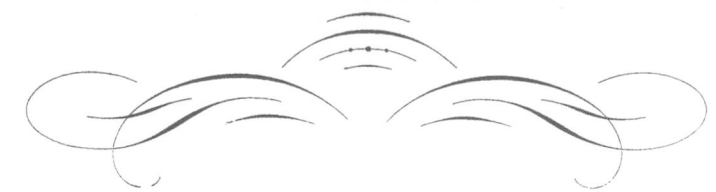

INDEX

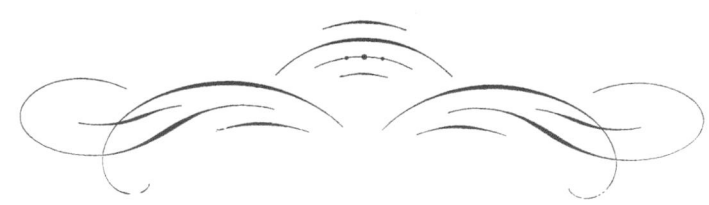

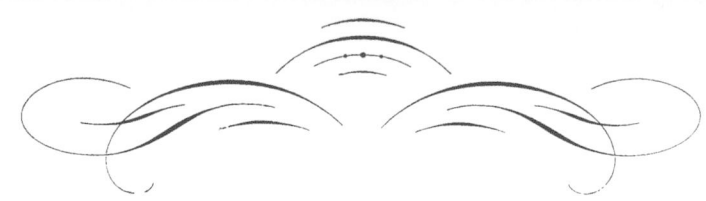

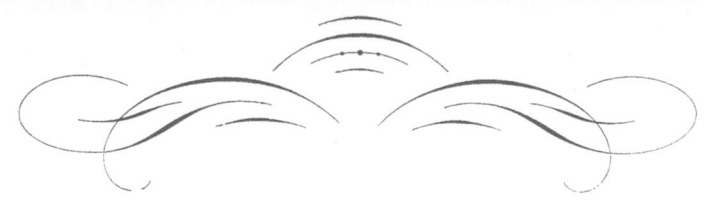

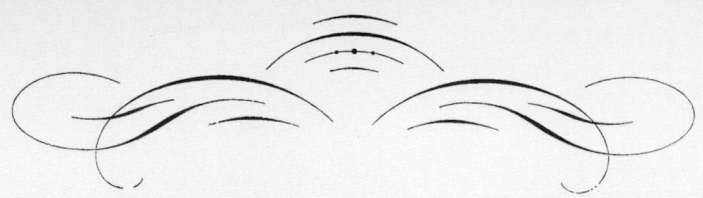

ACKNOWLEDGEMENTS

I've wanted to own this book ever since I started to cook, so I'm dead proud and very grateful that Kyle Cathie let me write it. Praise be to Georgia for breathing extraordinary life into it (it really is beyond the call of duty to work with your main squeeze) and to Daisy and Poppy not just for being in so many of her photos, but also for encouraging me to play with my food and for trying out so many of my hare-brained ideas. The only way that those ideas have taken book form is through the excitement, expertise and creativity of Jenny Wheatley, Marina Filippelli, Lindsay Milne Mcleod, Judith Hannam, Sue Prescott and Georgie Clarke, Two Associates, Laura Fyfe, Eve Teixeira and Amanda Booth.

I've genuinely spent years looking for the *Extraordinary Cookbook*, but it turned out that it didn't exist except in fragments in my fevered mind and scattered amongst the writings of a thousand brilliant writers from Brillat-Savarin to Heston Blumenthal, from Calvin H Schwabe to Hugh Fearnley-Whittingstall. So I'd like to say thank you to all the authors of the books, magazines, newspapers, TV and radio programmes whose ideas have inspired all this. I hope I haven't nicked anything wholesale!

Thanks to Jonathan Glynn-Smith for taking the suckling pig and author photos and to Fiona and Zoe Cox for letting us shoot crayfish, toffee apples and pumpkins at their beautiful house. Thanks to everyone who lent a little bit of their souls by appearing in the photos, especially Isaac and June, Alex (Zoe), Orlando (Hoops), Marni, Gabriel, Toby Farrant, Catharine, Eddie and Mark, Dora, Jo and Pia Glynn-Smith.

The following people helped to make this book either directly or indirectly, and whether they were aware of it or not: Borra Garson, Jan Croxon, Emma Hughes, Paul Gilheaney and all of the Gastronuts team at Objective and at the BBC, as well as all the brilliant kids who came on the show, the *Market Kitchen* team (especially the researchers), Andrea Sella, Will Daws, Kari Lia, Jack Storm, Karen O'Connor, Janice Hadlow, Gary Hunter, Bompass & Parr, Michelle Kass, Dora Hegyi, Nick Gibson, Chris Godfrey, Jean Gates, Nicky Ross, Harriet and Mark, Eric Gates, Anneka, Angus and Barney for the secret oyster hunt, Tom Gates, Thomas Cara, Jean-Anthelme and all my mates who've joined in these extraordinary feasts.